First State Plates:
Iconic Delaware Restaurants and Recipes

DELAWARE
CULINARY
TRAIL

Written by Pam George • Photography by Keith Mosher

I've been a cook, a chef, a general manager and a restaurant owner. I spent years working in the culinary melting pot of New Orleans, and I've traveled all over the world, enjoying everything from classic cuisine made using centuries-old techniques to cutting-edge dishes prepared by the hottest chefs.

Yet I am constantly bowled over by the diversity of dining that we have right here in Delaware.

Part of that has to do with our rich supply of natural resources. Delaware fronts the Atlantic Ocean and the Delaware Bay. Waterways lace the state from top to bottom. This is the place to find rockfish, oysters and steamed crabs.

Despite our urban and suburban areas in the north, we're still blessed with acres of farmland in the south, and you can witness their bounty at the many farmers markets throughout the state. Taste a tomato still warm from the sun, and butter sweet corn picked just that morning.

Sussex County produces more broiler chickens than any other county in the nation, and chicken is a staple on most menus, be it fried, roasted or served with the county's famous slippery dumplings. No matter where you dine, your meal will no doubt include local ingredients. Chefs here are natural advocates for sustainability; we began buying from local suppliers long before it became a national movement.

Because of our beach resorts, our global corporations and our proximity to major urban centers, our restaurants have a sophisticated, well-traveled clientele, and that's reflected on the menus throughout the state.

We're just as devoted to the places where you can grab a quick bite, namely Capriotti's Sandwich Shop, a home-grown success story, and Claymont Steak Shop. Both are places that Delawareans dream about when they're forced to relocate to other states. There are many others, including the Charcoal Pit, The Dog House and Sambo's Tavern. These established restaurants are part of many families' histories and traditions.

While Delaware's restaurants can hold their own against our big-city neighbors' eateries, we still manage to be approachable and unpretentious. You'll feel welcome when you pull up a chair, whether you're in a hip downtown eatery or in a down-home diner. That's just the Delaware way.

Harry's Savoy Grill is privileged and honored to be included in this book and on the Delaware Culinary Trail. We hope you enjoy the outstanding food in the First State.

Bon Appetit!

Xavier Teixido
Owner,
Harry's Savoy Grill

Living in Delaware and working in the state's tourism industry have made it clear to me that dining out is one of the top activities for residents and visitors here in the state.

Our fabulous collection of restaurants loudly states the obvious: Dining out should be spotlighted as a tourist attraction, too. And that's the idea behind the Delaware Culinary Trail.

The 24 restaurants you'll find in these pages offer just a sampling of the great tastes of the First State. From the Piedmont region of the northern part of the state to the coast line, there is a flavor to please everyone's palate on this menu-like road map of Delaware.

Delaware is known for high-quality poultry raised fresh; scrapple perfected through generations of down-home knowledge; and crabs and seafood caught in waters lauded for cleanliness. Our cuisine showcases these specialties at restaurants that are both local favorites and tourist attractions, whether it's a burger joint preserved through decades of change, fine-dining establishments boasting traditions of excellence or small-town restaurants that serve unique dishes born and bred in Delaware.

Delaware food is also about its people. Real people making real food and running small businesses that make eating out a top activity in Delaware. It's about extraordinary chefs and entrepreneurial visionaries delivering five-star food you'd expect to find in the big city without the big city prices.

From cracking open crabs with friends at Sambo's to savoring an elegant meal at the Hotel du Pont to basking in the sunset while noshing on fresh seafood at Bluecoast, the food is only part of the experience that is Delaware dining. Nowhere is that more evident than at our award-winning beaches, where you can dine and relax at one of several magnificent eateries along the Culinary Coast.

Delaware dining is also about life moments. With promises of excellence and a perfectly succulent prime rib, Harry's Savoy Grill has been the site of countless milestone anniversary dinners and celebrations. And at the Charcoal Pit, retro is reality as friends and families ditch the devices to devour mounds of ice cream, with the soundtrack provided by table-top jukeboxes.

Our state has so many remarkable restaurants that we easily could have rolled out a seafood, pizza or fine-dining trail. We chose these two dozen restaurants because we consider them to be icons of Delaware dining.

We hope you have enjoyed this journey through the Delaware Culinary Trail, and that you will explore the rest of the amazing restaurants, attractions and sites throughout our wonderful state.

Linda Parkowski
Director of Tourism,
State of Delaware

Printed in the United States of America

First Printing, 2013

ISBN 978-0-615-75117-7

Delaware Tourism Office
99 Kings Highway
Dover, DE 19901

www.visitdelaware.com

TABLE OF CONTENTS

DELAWARE CULINARY TRAIL

Harry's Savoy Grill

2020 Naamans Road

Wilmington, DE 19810

302.475.3000

www.harryshospitalitygroup.com

Wild About Harry: Harry's Savoy Grill

I f you live anywhere near north Wilmington, you'll likely wind up at Harry's Savoy Grill sooner or later. At least, that's been owner Xavier Teixido's experience. "You come here for a wedding, a shower, a meeting or a retirement dinner," he says. "You come to celebrate a birthday or anniversary. It's turned into the town hall of north Wilmington, and that's what Harry's Savoy Grill is all about."

Born in Paraguay, Teixido came to the United States with his family when he was 2. He worked in the restaurant industry in Philadelphia and New Orleans, where he met Emeril Lagasse. He returned to Delaware to join the 1492 Hospitality Group, which opened Harry's Savoy Grill in 1988.

The restaurant represented a return to the classics: chilled martinis, prime rib and Caesar salad, all served in an atmosphere reminiscent of an English men's club. (The "Savoy" in the name salutes The Savoy Grill in London.) Despite its time-honored take, Harry's Savoy Grill is typically ahead of the curve. Dishes showcase seasonal ingredients, and the restaurant, among the first to serve rare ahi tuna, is known for seafood. It's that blend of old-school cuisine and chef-driven selections that gives Harry's Savoy Grill a universal appeal.

Harry's Savoy Grill's name was inspired by artwork for the restaurant created by Harry McCormick. "We had never met a bad Harry," owner Xavier Teixido says. The name stuck, and the "Savoy" added a touch of class.

"We have a very diverse clientele," says Teixido, who has owned the restaurant on his own since 1993. Customers like the consistency and the comfortable atmosphere. Bartenders have worked here for years, and regulars park at the bar, which boasts a distinctive flared edge. A communal table stands near the bar, and when someone sits down, inevitably others call out "hello." "Our goal has always been to be a community steakhouse with a good, classic bar," Teixido says.

It is, however, so much more. The main dining room, where the prime rib takes center stage at a carving station, is a first-class location for special occasions. The slender Bacchus Room is a more intimate area for quiet conversation. In summer, diners request a spot on the covered patio. Teixido moves easily from room to room, wearing a constant smile beneath his signature mustache.

Although Harry's Hospitality Group now owns three other restaurants and the adjoining ballroom, the gregarious Teixido remains a frequent and familiar presence. His name is not above the restaurant door, and that's fine by him. Harry's Savoy Grill, which is located on a site occupied by hospitality venues since the 1940s, has its own identity. "We consider ourselves stewards of a legacy," he concludes.

Prime Rib with Potatoes au Gratin

Harry's Savoy Grill was founded to bring back the classics. Perhaps no dish is as classic as prime rib, which when grilled is known as a Delmonico. Buying a bone-in cut adds more flavor.

Serves: 10

Prep Time: 20 minutes

Cook Time: 3 hours

Serving Suggestion

▶ To make a clever "cup" for horseradish or a horseradish cream sauce, slice a cucumber into sections that are about 2 inches long. Score the sides, if you wish, to create stripes in the peel. Hollow them out and fill with horseradish or sauce. If you like a lot of sauce, make the cups longer.

Ingredient Substitution

▶ Use water in place of beef stock.

For the roast:

INGREDIENTS

1 10-pound bone-in prime rib roast
2 tablespoons of salt
2 tablespoons of black pepper
2 tablespoons of rosemary, fresh or dried
1 cup of celery, chopped
1 cup of onion, chopped
1 cup of carrot, chopped
1 quart of beef stock
Dash of Worcestershire sauce

PREPARATION

1. Rub the salt, pepper and rosemary over the roast.

2. Place vegetables in a roasting pan and place the roast on the vegetables.

3. Roast for 30 minutes in a preheated 400-degree oven.

4. Reduce heat to 200 degrees and roast for 2 hours or until the meat's internal temperature reaches 130 degrees.

5. Remove the roast from the oven and let it rest until it's medium rare.

6. Place the roasting pan with the drippings and vegetables on the stove.

7. Add beef stock.

8. Simmer for 30 minutes or until liquid is reduced by half.

9. Check seasonings and add salt and pepper if needed.

10. Add the Worcestershire sauce.

11. Strain and reserve the sauce.

12. Slice the meat, plate and ladle the sauce on top.

For the potatoes au gratin:

INGREDIENTS

4 ounces of whole butter
2 tablespoons of fresh thyme, leaves removed from stem
1 firmly packed cup of leeks, white part only, washed and diced
5 large russet potatoes, peeled
Salt and pepper to taste.
1 quart of half-and-half
1 cup of grated Swiss cheese

PREPARATION

1. Melt butter in a saucepan, and add leeks and thyme.

2. Add potatoes and half-and-half.

3. Boil uncovered until the cream is a thick consistency and potatoes are tender.

4. Add salt and pepper.

5. Place in a casserole dish and top with Swiss cheese.

6. Cook in a preheated 375-degree oven until golden brown.

Claymont Steak Shop

3526 Philadelphia Pike
Claymont, DE 19703
302.798.0013
www.claymontsteakshop.com

A Mouthwatering Mecca: Claymont Steak Shop

I t's 10 a.m., still two hours from lunch. But the aroma of rib-eye and fried onions on the commercial griddle is intoxicating. Using a spatula, the cook deftly moves the paper-thin slices of meat around the griddle. He folds in the onions and then American cheese. In minutes, he's ready to slip the mix into a roll—which is a good thing. Despite the hour, customers are already waiting, and the phone is ringing with lunchtime orders.

This is Claymont Steak Shop, a brick building that hugs the sidewalk in the small town off I-495 and I-95. A Delaware institution, the sandwich and pizza shop draws as many blue-collar workers as it does doctors and lawyers.

It's easy to see why the scent of steak, onions and pizza is so appealing to customers. Yet owner Demi Kollias is just as enticed. "That smells good, doesn't it?" she says.

Her uncle Bob Hionis and Sam Demetratos founded Claymont Steak in 1966. The cousins, who came to America from Greece, remembered the hunger that plagued their native country after World War II. "If they had the opportunity to own a business, they wanted to feed people—that's why we are so generous with the portions," Kollias says.

The packed sandwich is one reason why people willingly travel many miles to eat at Claymont Steak. Diehard customers say the quality of the meat is another. The shop uses always fresh—never frozen—rib-eye steak that's well-marbled for flavor. The oh-so-tender meat is sliced, not chopped. The rolls are also top shelf; a bakery makes them to the shop's specifications. "If they're not right, we send them back," Kollias says.

The shop originally held a counter and a few stools. When a neighboring drugstore and cleaners closed, Claymont Steak expanded. Today, the neat dining room holds colorful gumball machines, video arcade games and shiny bags of Herr's chips.

With 12 years of experience owning 7-11 franchises, Kollias purchased the shop in 2005. A Newark location opened in 2012, so customers traveling north could get their fix faster.

FUN FACT:

✶

At any given time during the day, a foot-high mound of sliced rib-eye stands on the side of the griddle. The meat is never "portioned" into a roll. Cooks just pack the roll to capacity.

✶

In Philly, customers order steaks "wit' Whiz." At Claymont Steak, American is the norm, but you can also get Swiss, provolone and, most recently, pepper jack. "You have to satisfy the customers' tastes," Kollias notes. Judging by the 10 a.m. throng, Claymont Steak Shop is doing just that.

Steak Sandwich with Cheese and Onions

Steak sandwich fans in the Delaware region can debate the merits of a good cheesesteak for seemingly hours. Everyone has a favorite, whether it's topped with Cheese Whiz or American cheese. There are articles written about it and blogs devoted to it. Most will agree that it starts with high-quality meat and a good roll.

Serves: 2

Prep Time:
5 minutes

Cook Time:
10 minutes

INGREDIENTS

2 ½ teaspoons of vegetable or olive oil

⅛ cup of diced onions

½ pound of fresh rib-eye steak, sliced very thin (ask your butcher to do this)

3 slices of American cheese or the cheese of your choice

1 steak roll, sliced in half lengthwise

PREPARATION

1. Add oil to a sauté pan and cook onions until translucent. Reserve.

2. Heat a Teflon pan until it's very hot. Add the meat. Move the meat around until it is cooked to your liking.

3. Fold in the onions and blend.

4. Top with the cheese. As it starts to melt, blend it into the steak-onion mix.

5. With a spatula, scoop the meat into the roll.

Serving Suggestion

▶ Offer ketchup, which is traditional at Claymont Steak Shop. Sautéed mushrooms and hot and sweet peppers are other common accoutrements.

SUCCESS TIPS

- As you cook the meat, look for any gristle, and discard it.
- Well-marbled meat has the best flavor.
- Claymont Steak sells both meat and rolls separately for those who want to make the sandwiches at home.
- If you're worried the meat will stick, add a small amount of water.
- Purchase a roll that is firm but not crunchy on the outside. You want it to support the meat but still be easy to eat.

Charcoal Pit

2600 Concord Pike

Wilmington, DE 19803

302.478.2165

www.charcoalpit.net

Blast from the Past: Charcoal Pit

nitially, it looks like a mirage. How could a restaurant remain so untouched for nearly 60 years, right down to the neon pink sign? If Fonzie and his friends suddenly appeared from under the round striped awning, it wouldn't be surprising.

That "Back to the Future" sensation only increases once you go inside. Mini silver jukeboxes stocked with oldies sit at most of the booths. A sign shaped like a soup bowl announces today's selection, and soda jerks are either elbow-deep in the ice cream case or topping hot fudge sundaes with a pyramid of whipped cream.

FUN FACT:

✶

The Charcoal Pit appears in Michael and Jane Stern's book "Roadfood: The Coast-to-Coast Guide to 600 of the Best Barbecue Joints, Lobster Shacks, Ice Cream Parlors, Highway Diners & Much, Much More."

✶

This is no retro fabrication. Opened in 1956, the Charcoal Pit is the place that time happily left intact. Just ask manager Frank Kucharski, who started as a dishwasher in 1969 and worked his way up from the ice cream station to the grill, where cooks flip 4-ounce and 8-ounce burgers.

Take a panoramic gaze at the walls and you'll see photos from the '50s when this was one of just a few businesses on a now-bustling strip and decades-old news clippings detailing the storied history of this hallowed hang-out.

The "Pit" has always been the place where pony-tailed girls gathered with football players after the big game, Kucharski recalls. Today, you'll still find gaggles of long-legged high-school girls and their boyfriends giggling over the Kitchen Sink, which has 20 scoops of ice cream, or one of nine sundaes named after and inspired by local high school teams. You'll also find the adult versions of the kids who grew up coming here. Some are married with kids—or grandkids.

In addition to the ice cream, another must-try is the Pit Special: a grilled burger topped with crisp lettuce, tomato, onion and pickles. It comes with a pleated paper cup of relish, made in house. Pair it with a shake, which still comes in a tall silver cup with a long-handled spoon.

The Pit was started by the Sloan brothers: Sam, Marty, Lou and Aaron, who also started The Dog House in New Castle. Louis Capano Jr. purchased the restaurant in the mid-1980s.

There is another Charcoal Pit location on Kirkwood Highway at Prices Corner, which is also a sports bar. Purists, however, line up at the North Wilmington site for burgers, cheesesteaks and ice cream, all served with a side of mid-20th century atmosphere.

As the Charcoal Pit demonstrates, some things should never change.

The Kitchen Sink

The Charcoal Pit is famous for its burgers, but its sign along Route 202 also touts "Ice Cream Creations," including black-and-white shakes, hot fudge sundaes and this behemoth, the Kitchen Sink, a memory-maker that's part of most residents' childhoods.

Serves: 4-8

Prep Time: 15 minutes

INGREDIENTS
7 scoops of chocolate ice cream
6 scoops of strawberry ice cream
7 scoops of vanilla ice cream
1 jar of wet walnuts
1 jar of crushed cherries
1 jar of crushed pineapple
Chocolate syrup to taste
1 can of whipped cream
Two bananas, quartered into "spears"
7 cherries

PREPARATION
1. Add the scoops in any arrangement in a bowl large enough to hold them.
2. Add each topping in order, using as much or as little as you wish.
3. Make seven mounds of whipped cream.
4. Top each with a cherry.
5. Decorate with the bananas.

SUCCESS TIPS

• The whipped cream should blanket the ice cream. To show off your concoction to your guests, add the topping at the table.

DELAWARE
CULINARY
TRAIL

Green Room at Hotel du Pont

11th & Market Streets

Wilmington, DE 19801

302.594.3154

www.hoteldupont.com/green-room-en.html

The Age of Elegance: Green Room

I n 1956, when Rosalind Russell was appearing in "Auntie Mame" at the DuPont Theatre (then the Playhouse Theatre), she decided to dine in the Green Room, which is also in the Hotel du Pont. As the statuesque Russell entered the dining room, the diners pushed back their chairs and gave her a standing ovation. It was, she later recalled, the only time she'd received one in a restaurant.

It's not surprising that the restaurant's guests would recognize and applaud talent. The symbol for fine dining in Delaware—and, indeed, the region—the Green Room upholds the traditions of the early 20th century, an opulent era captured so well on the BBC series "Downton Abbey." Polished service, exquisitely prepared food and luxurious appointments were the hallmark of an exceptional hotel.

Over the years, the Green Room and the hotel have experienced updates, but renovations in the past 10 years have restored its original grandeur. In the dining room, carved oak paneling reflects the shimmering lights of crystal-and-gold chandeliers, which dangle from a two-story coffered ceiling over white tablecloths.

The cuisine is still considered French—you'd expect nothing less—but served on Versace china. Yet the menu is hardly mired in the past. Seared Hudson Valley foie gras might come with maple syrup, cranberry jam and a toasted pumpkin-spiced brioche. Duck breast is accompanied by pork belly, French lentils and Swiss chard. Chilean sea bass is livened by Sauternes-beurre blanc yet served with charred corn-and-garlic grits. The kitchen keeps it creative and seasonal. Expect plenty of butternut squash, pumpkin and cold weather greens in fall, for instance.

The hotel is the vision of Pierre S. du Pont, a former DuPont Co. president, who wanted it to compete with the best European properties. Since opening in 1913, the hotel has hosted such luminaries as Prince Rainer of Monaco, John F. Kennedy Jr. and Norman Rockwell. Many undoubtedly dined in the Green Room. Thanks to the theater, you might spot a performer. Even the celebrities can be surprised. During the filming of a cooking segment, Julia Child reached up to touch a stack of plates on the brunch buffet when a waiter slapped her hand in rebuke. The startled Child turned to find comedian Tim Conway, posing as a waiter to surprise his friend.

There are many stories of romantic meals between celebrities and Delaware socialites. But the staff is mum. In the Green Room, good manners always prevail.

FUN FACT:

No one is sure how the Green Room, originally known as the Main Dining Room, got its name. Some credit Helena Springer Green who, with her husband, John J. Raskob, kept a suite at the hotel. Others say the original décor was predominantly green.

French Breast of Chicken, Sautéed Foie Gras, Grilled Pineapple, Smoked Blueberry Sauce and Meyer Lemon Gastrique

The jewel in Delaware's culinary crown, The Green Room is Delaware's premier restaurant, and this sophisticated dish demonstrates why.

Serves: 4
Prep Time: 30 minutes
Cook Time: 1 hour

INGREDIENTS

1 golden pineapple
2 pints of blueberries
4 shallots
8 ounces of port
2 ounces of honey
1 ounce of red wine vinegar
6 Meyer lemons
6 ounces of apple-honey vinegar
1 ½ cups of granulated sugar
16 ounces of chicken stock
1 butternut squash, peeled and small diced
4 6-8 ounces French breast of chicken, skin on, winglet trimmed
Salt and pepper
4 ounces of butter, cold and cubed
2 sprigs of thyme
2 sprigs of rosemary
4 2-ounce portions of foie gras
2 ounces of vegetable or canola oil

PREPARATION

1. Peel the pineapple, and cut into ¼-inch rings. Core and remove the centers. Cut each ring into quarter moons. Reserve.

2. Smoke the blueberries in a smoker or on your gas grill with hickory or apple wood chips for 30 minutes.

3. Mince one shallot. Add to a sauté pan with the port, and reduce by half.

4. Add the honey and smoked blueberries, reduce by ⅔.

5. Puree in a blender.

6. Add 1 ounce of red wine vinegar, strain to remove the fruit skins and keep warm. Reserve the sauce.

7. Zest three of the Meyer lemons, and juice all 6. Reserve.

8. Combine 6 ounces of apple-honey vinegar and the granulated sugar in a pot. Cook until it's a golden brown caramel.

9. Remove from heat and carefully add the Meyer lemon juice and zest, stirring constantly. Keep warm.

10. Bring stock to a boil. Reduce to medium heat, and add diced squash. Cook until the squash is tender.

11. Strain and keep the squash warm.

12. Roughly chop the remaining shallots.

13. Season the chicken breasts with salt and pepper to taste.

14. Heat a sauté pan on high, add 1 ounce of butter. Swirl the pan.

15. Add chicken breasts, skin side down and sear to a golden brown. Flip the chicken, and add remaining cubed butter, the roughly chopped shallots, thyme and rosemary sprigs.

16. Baste the skin side of the chicken breasts with the butter in the pan. (Use a spoon.) Place in a preheated 350-degree oven, and cook until the meat's internal temperature reaches 150 degrees.

17. Remove from the oven, and let the chicken rest 10 minutes.

18. Crosshatch the top of foie gras, and season with salt and pepper.

19. Place foie gras crosshatched side down in a clean sauté pan on medium-high heat. Cook until the crosshatched side is brown. Flip, and cook 3 minutes, basting the fat over the foie gras.

20. Remove from the pan, and place on paper towels.

21. Lightly oil and then grill the pineapple half moons on both sides.

22. Remove from grill.

TO PLATE

1. Place diced squash in 3-inch ring mold in center of the plate, and press to firm up the squash. Remove the mold.

2. Lean chicken breast on the squash.

3. Place four pineapple half moons in a circular pattern next to the chicken.

4. Place foie gras on top of the pineapple.

5. Pour both the blueberry and Meyer lemon sauces next to each other in front and around chicken.

SUCCESS TIPS

- Smoke the blueberries in advance, and puree and heat just before serving.

- Make the Meyer lemon gastrique in advance, and reheat.

- Grill the pineapple the day before, then reheat in the oven before serving.

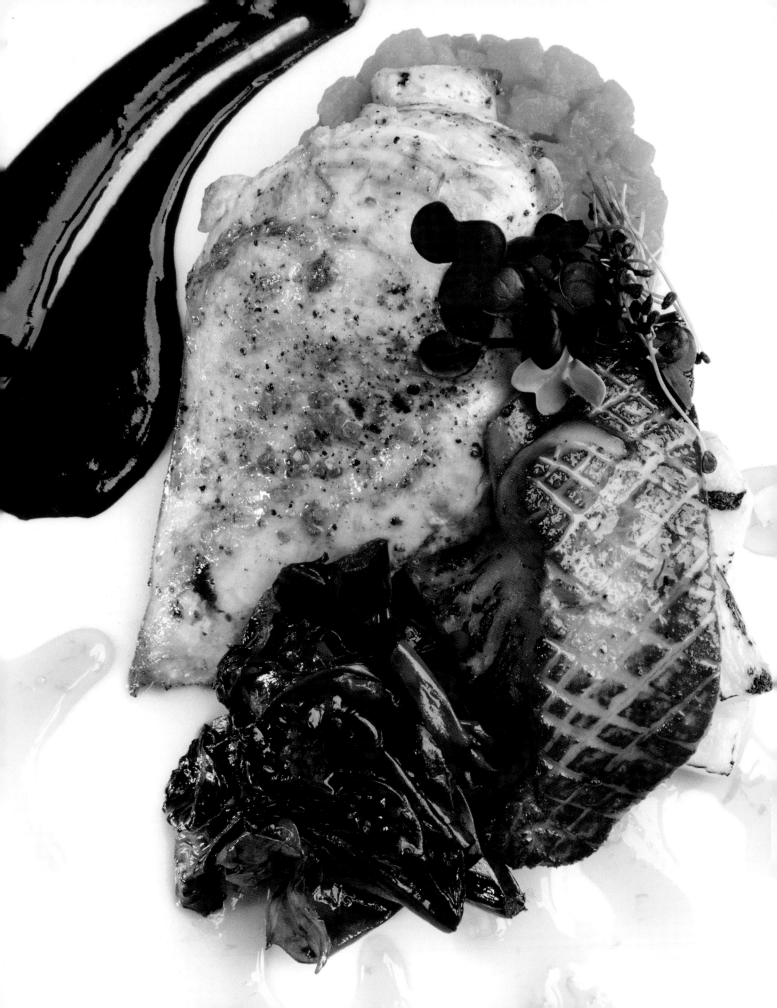

Piccolina Toscana

1412 North Dupont Street

Wilmington, DE 19806

302.654.8001

www.piccolinatoscana.com

The Heartbeat of Trolley Square: Piccolina Toscana

There are those who say you shouldn't mess with success. And then there is Dan Butler. Since opening his first restaurant in 1991, he's given it some serious tweaks. Born as Griglia Toscana, which brought an urban attitude to Trolley Square, it then became Tavola Toscana, followed by Toscana Kitchen + Bar, which signified the addition of a happening lounge. The most recent makeover, which included a fresh decor and new menu, turned the space into Piccolina Toscana.

Changing this neighborhood restaurant even a bit could spell disaster. It's packed with memories for hundreds of Delaware diners. But Butler, a Wilmington native and Culinary Institute of America graduate, has an uncanny knack for knowing what his customers want, what they want to pay and what's hot on the culinary scene. As the chef puts it: "Times change, and sometimes you change with them and sometimes you help them change."

Butler knew he wanted to be a chef before he ever boiled water. At age 16, he saw a TV program on the Culinary Institute of America. A family friend was a CIA graduate. That's all it took. "I was going to conquer the culinary world," he says. A dishwashing job at the Hotel du Pont and home economic classes at St. Mark's High School put him on the path.

After graduating from the CIA, Butler got a job at a Washington, D.C., restaurant focusing on northern Italian food. At the time, most Italian eateries were serving red gravy. "It made a big impression on me," Butler says. He worked in Miami for the same owner, and then headed to Tampa, where he helped open three northern Italian restaurants.

FUN FACT:

Piccolina means "little girl" or "little one" in Italian. It signifies Toscana's promotion of the small plate concept.

Butler knew he would return to Wilmington. "I always felt like Wilmington was my home; I speak the language," he says. A vacancy in the Rockford Shops gave him the opportunity to start his own business.

His current menu includes small- or full-sized options. To sample several dishes, order a small plate of braised beef short rib-filled pasta with mushroom and red wine demi-glace followed by potato dumplings with sage-scented veal Bolognese sauce. Or, order a full-size portion of one or the other. There are traditional-size entrees (grilled filet medallions over cannellini bean puree), salads and small or large pasta portions. Pizzas, made in the wood-burning oven, have been a staple since the start.

The restaurant's new rustic look was inspired by a loft. Think painted brick, rescued barn wood and oversized art panels. A recipe in Italian is scrawled across a chalkboard mural.

The open dining room fits Delaware to a T: You can see and be seen with ease. And one of those Dele-brities will undoubtedly be Butler himself, even though he has a busy catering unit and three other local restaurants—and counting. No matter how stressed he is, Butler appears at ease, unflappable and sociable. He's rarely at a loss for words—or a clever sense of humor.

By now, most frequent customers just call the restaurant "Toscana." The updated name décor are appreciated, but it's the consistency and community that prompts return visits. The more things change, the more they stay the same.

Tortellini with Mortadella, Ham and Ricotta in a Sun-Dried Tomato and Cream Sauce

Piccolina Toscana's décor and menu have received regular updates since it opened in 1991, but this dish remains a consistent favorite.

Serves: 4

Prep Time: 1 hour

Cook Time: 20 minutes

For the filling:

INGREDIENTS
4 ounces of ham
4 ounces of mortadella
1 ounce of grated Reggiano cheese
4 ounces of whole milk ricotta cheese
1 tablespoon of chopped parsley

PREPARATION
1. Grind the meat together in a meat grinder or food processor.
2. Mix with the other ingredients.
3. Refrigerate.

For the pasta:

INGREDIENTS
3-4 large eggs, beaten
10 ounces of high-gluten flour
Special equipment: Pasta machine, tabletop mixer with a dough hook

PREPARATION
1. Combine most of the beaten eggs (reserve some to add later if needed) and flour using a tabletop mixer with a dough hook attachment, and beat until it forms a ball. (You may need more egg to form the ball.)

2. Remove from the machine and knead 15-20 minutes.
3. Cover with plastic wrap and let rest for 30 minutes until it becomes pliable.

For the tortellini:

INGREDIENTS
Filling
Dough
Semolina flour
Salt

PREPARATION
1. Cut a piece of the rested dough and roll it through the pasta-rolling machine, set on the thinnest setting, to make one long sheet of pasta.
2. Quickly cut 1 ½-inch circles from the sheet.
3. Place a dollop of the meat mixture in the center of each.
4. Fold one edge of the pasta over the meat to meet the other edge, creating a half moon.
5. Pick the pasta up, and curl it around your finger.
6. Dust with semolina flour and refrigerate until ready to use.
7. Cook pasta in boiling salted water for 4 minutes until it floats to the surface.
8. Plunge into the simmering sun-dried tomato-cream sauce.

For the sauce:

INGREDIENTS
16 ounces of heavy cream
2 ounces of Reggiano
1 tablespoon of cornstarch
Water
4 tablespoons of sun-dried tomatoes, finely chopped
Salt and pepper

PREPARATION
1. Heat the cream in a saucepan.
2. Whisk in the cheese, and bring to a boil.
3. Put cornstarch in a cup, and add just enough water to give it a glue-like consistency.
4. Add the cornstarch to the cream and bring to a boil, stirring. The sauce should thicken.
5. Add the sun-dried tomatoes and season as needed.

SUCCESS TIPS

- Work very quickly when making the tortellini or the dough will dry out and crack.
- You can buy top-quality tortellini and just make the sauce if you're pressed for time.

Walter's Steakhouse

802 North Union Street

Wilmington, DE 19805

302.652.6780

www.walters-steakhouse.com

The Beef Goes On: Walter's Steakhouse

At age 14, John Walter Constantinou stepped up to the cutting table at his father's restaurant, Constantinou's House of Beef, and it was love at first slice. But when people asked him if he wanted to take over the restaurant when he grew up, the teen hesitated.

"My father worked seven days a week, 12 hours a day," he recalls. Indeed, Constantinou's was a fixture in Trolley Square from 1959 to 1986, and the gregarious George Constantinou, who came to America from Greece at age 14, was a large part of its success. "He liked steakhouse customers; they were businesspeople and extroverts—the type of people my father enjoys," his son says.

But after the restaurant closed and John Constantinou pursued a career in real estate, he found his eye wandering to the listings of available restaurant properties.

In 1993, Constantinou opened Walter's Steakhouse in Wilmington's Little Italy section.

FUN FACT:
✦
Walter's is located in a former bar—the first to get a liquor license in Wilmington after Prohibition ended.
✦

The restaurant, which can proudly call itself "Wilmington's oldest steakhouse," has a comfortable atmosphere that's part Victorian and part club. Dressed in burgundy and hunter green, the rooms feature exposed red brick, rich wood trim and light fixtures that salute the late 19th century. The look suits this established section of the city. Sit around the bar and you'll feel the whisper of old Wilmington throughout the space.

The quiet-spoken, even-keeled Constantinou, who regularly takes to the floor to greet guests, has fostered a friendly environment that's a welcome departure from some urban steakhouse chains. Happy hour specials and daily bar menu offerings bring the faithful back on a regular basis. A strong believer in value, he offers a salad and potato with entrées.

Because the name is so well known in Wilmington, many longtime Delawareans call the restaurant Constantinou's. That's fine by Constantinou. In fact, it's high praise. He's never regretted his choice to follow in his father's footsteps. "There's a certain amount of satisfaction you get from a career when you enjoy the work," he says.

Bone-In Rib-Eye with Mashed Root Vegetables

Some call it a Delmonico. Others call it a rib-eye. And if you roast it, it's prime rib. Any steak with a bone gets a boost of flavor, so this recipe delivers a double whammy. Root vegetables are a novel replacement for the usual baked potato.

Serves: 2

Prep Time:
15 minutes

Cook Time:
35 minutes

For the steaks:

INGREDIENTS

2 bone-in rib-eye steaks, about
1 ¼-1 ½-inch thick each
Canola oil, enough to brush the steaks
Salt and pepper to taste
Aged balsamic vinegar

PREPARATION

1. Lightly brush the steaks with the oil then liberally salt and pepper each one. Place a cast-iron frying pan over high heat and get the pan very hot.

2. Add the steaks and sear about 3-4 minutes on each side.

3. Finish on the grill to your desired temperature.

4. Before serving, lightly drizzle aged balsamic vinegar over the steak to taste.

For the root vegetables:

INGREDIENTS

1 medium turnip
1 medium parsnip or 2 small parsnips
3 Yukon Gold potatoes
½ cup of heavy cream or less
3 tablespoons of butter
Salt and pepper to taste

PREPARATION

1. Peel the vegetables and chop them into pieces.

2. Place them all in salted water. Bring to a boil and cook for about 20 minutes or until tender. Drain.

3. Combine the vegetables with butter and cream—use the cream sparingly and add as needed so you don't have too much liquid.

4. With a hand mixer or masher, mash or whip the vegetables.

5. Salt and pepper to taste.

Serving Suggestion

► For a vegetable, consider grilled asparagus tossed in olive oil.

SUCCESS TIPS

• Use a meat thermometer to make sure the steak is done to your liking.
• Angle the steaks on the grill for attractive stripe marks that run on a diagonal.

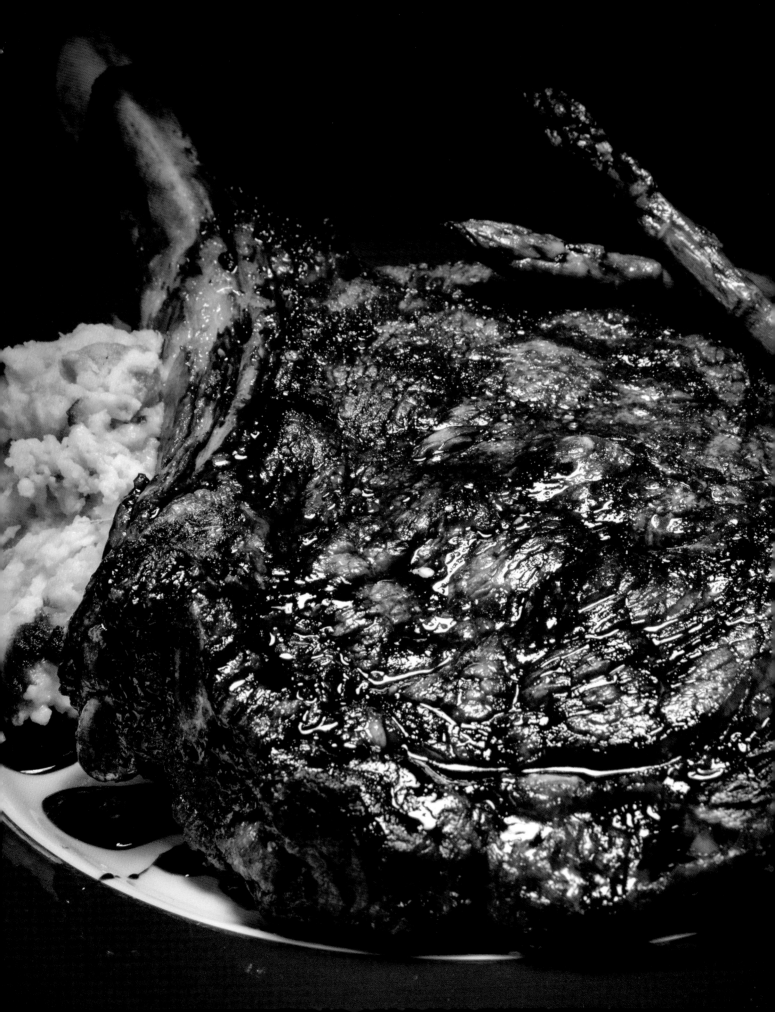

The Dog House
1200 North Dupont Highway
New Castle, DE 19720
302.328.5380

An All-American Icon: The Dog House

Patience is a virtue at The Dog House. During peak periods, diners who want to eat-in need to hover in the back, eyes trained on the 17 counter stools. An occupant barely has time to stand before a newcomer nabs the vacant seat.

Savvy customers determine what they want before sitting down. That's because it only takes a few seconds for a server to ask for your order. Then watch your split foot-long dog hit the grill across from you and start to sizzle under a steak weight. It's not long before the hotdog and all the trimmings—chili and onions are a must—are casually delivered to you in plain wrapping.

The grill is the star here. Along with hotdogs, which can also include sauerkraut or the "works," the tiny restaurant cooks up burgers, steak sandwiches and grilled cheese. However, roast turkey sandwiches, made with turkey that's roasted on-site each day, also get a thumbs up from fans. Crisp French fries with seasoning are the must-do side dish.

This is a lively place where conversation is king, and the train car-like space is slender enough to guarantee that you'll never eat alone.

The bustle, the elbow-to-elbow crowd, and the kitchen action are all part of the experience at The Dog House. Darlene Spence should know. She's been employed here for nearly 25 years. Her father, Mitch "Hut" Reinhart, was 13 when he began working here, and he never left. When the original owner, Lou Sloan, put it up for sale in February 2012, father and daughter jumped at the chance to own it.

They've seen a lot of familiar faces over the years. Spence instantly remembered the onetime regulars who returned unexpectedly. Turns out they'd moved to Ohio. "They were here for two weeks, and they ate lunch here every day," Spence says.

FUN FACT:

★

The Dog House was founded by the Sloan brothers, who also started the Charcoal Pit in north Wilmington. Both spots are known for their retro appeal.

★

Seven Washington, D.C., doctors and their wives go on road trips just to eat at The Dog House. A Dover family comes once a month. Not all the faithful come in cars. A Connecticut developer flew into the New Castle County Airport, located down the highway, to pick up 80 sandwiches and fly home.

The hotdogs, served on rolls made for the restaurant, are a draw. But customers also love that the menu and the atmosphere have remained the same throughout The Dog House's 60-plus years. "Nothing has changed," Spence says. Well, she amends, except the addition of the turkey sandwiches.

There are always new faces. "We're seeing our fourth generation of customers: the parents, the kids, the grandchildren and now the great-grandchildren," Spence says.

In New Castle, biting into your first chilidog is a delicious rite of passage.

The Dog House with "Everything"

When you're "in the doghouse" it's a good thing at the New Castle eatery with the memorable name. The Dog House is famous for its foot-long hotdogs. If you can find that length in the store, buy them instead of the standard hotdogs.

Serves: 8

Prep Time:
10 minutes

Cook Time:
5-10 minutes

INGREDIENTS

1 ½ tomatoes, cut in slices
12 slices of American cheese (optional)
1 8-pack of Dietz & Watson hotdogs
8 hotdog rolls
Ketchup and mustard to taste
1 small onion, chopped
¼ head of lettuce, chopped
¼ cup of cabbage, chopped fine

PREPARATION

1. Cut the tomato slices in half.
2. Cut each slice of cheese in half.
3. Split the hotdogs down the middle.
4. Put hotdogs skinside down on a hot frying pan or grill.
5. Cook until brown and flip.
6. Cook until lightly browned.
7. Add three of the halved cheese slices to the hotdog and let them melt.
8. Lightly toast the rolls.
9. Spread ketchup and mustard on the inside of each roll.
10. Add the hotdogs.
11. Place tomato slices on the roll.
12. Add a sprinkling of chopped onions.
13. Put a small amount of the lettuce and cabbage on each hotdog.

SUCCESS TIPS

• The secret ingredient is the cabbage, so don't leave it out.

Serving Suggestion

▶ Serve the hotdogs with French fries dusted with Morton Season Salt, the closest seasoning you'll find to the spice mix that The Dog House uses.

Deer Park Tavern

108 West Main Street

Newark, DE 19711

302.369.9414

www.deerparktavern.com

A National Treasure: Deer Park Tavern

On a Saturday night, traffic on the one-way Main Street in Newark is stop-and-go. There's activity on both the street and sidewalks. Families, holding gelato cones, stroll past boutiques, while University of Delaware students pop into gathering spots for a cold beer. Under awnings, couples crowd al fresco tables.

Many will wind up at the Deer Park, a three-and-a-half-story beacon at West Main Street and New London Road. While the college campus and the downtown area define Newark, the Deer Park, built in 1851, is the place where students, residents and alumni come together as one. "Everybody has a story about the Deer Park," says Sandy Ashby.

That includes Ashby. In 1974, while attending UD, she spotted Bob Ashby at a football game. "I thought he was adorable," she recalls. "I said: 'Who is that guy? I'm going to marry him.'" They ran into each other at the Deer Park Tavern, then a watering hole that smelled of stale beer. "He thought he was hot stuff," she jokes. She told him he was conceited and promptly fell off her barstool. They've been together ever since.

Before they married, the Ashbys both worked at H.A. Winston & Co. in Wilmington, where he became part-owner. In 1983, the Ashbys purchased the old Drummond Ale House in Newark, another haunt from their college days, and turned it into McGlynns Pub & Restaurant. There are now two other locations. In 2001, they bought the Deer Park.

"It was such a huge and frightening project," she says. Despite being listed in the National Register of Historic Places, it had fallen into disrepair. Using a vintage postcard, Bob Ashby oversaw its complete renovation, right down to the porch spindles. He helped dig the elevator shaft.

The Deer Park's site was previously occupied by the St. Patrick's Inn. Along with Edgar Allen Poe, George Washington, Charles Mason and Jeremiah Dixon (creators of the Mason-Dixon line) visited the inn. The Deer Park has been an inn, a women's seminary, a brothel, a polling place, a ballroom, a barbershop, a liquor store and a Chinese restaurant.

The Deer Park still caters to a mostly college crowd with an affordable menu that includes burgers, nachos, sandwiches and flatbread pizza. Yet sauces and stocks are made from scratch, and steaks are high quality. The upstairs banquet rooms have been used for fraternity and sorority rushes, faculty parties and UD and Newark High School alumni events.

It's now common to see families in the updated dining room. "Generations of folks enjoy bringing their offspring back to the place of their glory days," Bob Ashby says.

Los Nachos Grande

Few dishes lend themselves to a social occasion as well as a big plate of nachos, and Los Nachos Grande has been a tradition at the Deer Park through several ownerships. It's the classic bar nosh.

Serves: 2-4

Prep Time:
10 minutes

Cook Time:
5-8 minutes

INGREDIENTS

1 large bag of triangle-shaped tortilla chips
16 ounces of shredded Monterey Jack cheese
8 ounces of hot chili
4-6 ounces of shredded iceberg lettuce
4-6 ounces of diced tomatoes
3 ounces of sour cream
4 ounces of sliced jalapeños

PREPARATION

1. Place half the nachos in a layer on an ovenproof plate large enough to hold them.
2. Spread half the cheese on top of the nachos.
3. Repeat with a layer of nachos and another layer of cheese.
4. Place the plate in a preheated 350-degree oven, and bake until the cheese melts.
5. Remove the plate and ladle the chili over the melted cheese and chips.
6. Sprinkle lettuce and tomatoes on top.
7. Add a dollop of sour cream, and top the entire dish with jalapeños.

SUCCESS TIPS

• Make sure the nachos are large and flat enough to overlap and support the toppings.

Serving Suggestion

▶ Include a variety of Mexican beers for a tasting.

▶ Offer black olives or scallions on the side.

Smyrna Diner

99 South Cory Lane

Smyrna, DE 19977

302.653.9980

www.smyrnadiner.net

Comfort Food Served with a Smile: Smyrna Diner

It's 6 a.m., and Jamie Compton is already at work, opening the doors of the Smyrna Diner to waiting customers. Some want a hot cup of coffee for the road. Situated just off Delaware's main traffic artery, the diner is a rest stop unto itself popular with travelers and truck drivers who want a quick bite. Others want heartier fare: scrapple and eggs, creamed beef over toast with home fries or corned beef hash and eggs. The enticing smell of bacon, coffee and frying eggs greets the newcomers as soon as they walk inside the restaurant.

FUN FACT:

★

Loretta Lynn, Robert Plant and Joe Pesci are just a few of the celebrities who've eaten at Smyrna Diner.

★

It's been the same scene nearly every morning since 1956, when the Smyrna Diner opened its doors. The diner is part of many collective communities' memories, from Middletown to Odessa to Smyrna to Dover. "Great eats," residents will say with a sigh of nostalgia. Others know the diner as the traditional pit stop when they traveled from northern Delaware to the beaches in the pre-Route 1 days.

Compton grew up in the business. She was 2 when her mother took over the restaurant, and it wasn't long before she was peeling potatoes and busing tables. And in 2008, when the Smyrna Diner moved on from its long-time home to a new building, Compton moved along with it, buying the restaurant with her husband, Jonathan. She has known some of the staff since she was a child. "Since then we've added more wonderful people who've helped us become a successful, iconic restaurant," she says.

Just like the old days, the Smyrna Diner continues to be a family business. Compton lives a few minutes from the restaurant, and she and her husband make sure at least one of them is there at all times. Their three children have all worked in the diner, including the youngest, who is 12.

The familiar faces have eased the transition for regulars who needed to acclimate to the new space. So has the familiar menu. The diner is still celebrated for homemade chicken and dumplings, served on Tuesday and Friday; biscuits with sausage gravy; and chicken croquettes topped with turkey gravy. Eggs are often accompanied with scrapple or pork roll. "There are many travelers who've never heard of these dishes," Compton says.

The building might be new, but the attitude remains the same. Says Compton: "It is an authentic 'diner' experience: great home cooking, great service and great value."

Scrapple, Egg & Cheese Sandwich

Cross the Chesapeake & Delaware Canal into Kent County and you're in scrapple country. Scrapple is made from meat "scraps," generally pork pieces, combined with cornmeal, wheat flour and spices. The cooked mix is formed into a loaf, and devotees panfry slices.

Serves: 1

Prep Time:
5 minutes

Cook Time:
10 minutes

INGREDIENTS

2 eggs
Cooking spray
1 teaspoon of vegetable oil
½-inch slice of scrapple
1 slice of American cheese or your favorite cheese, such as cheddar
1 bagel of your choice, sliced in half

PREPARATION

1. Spray a Teflon sauté pan with cooking spray.
2. Fry both sides of eggs to desired consistency.
3. Top the eggs with the cheese.
4. In a separate frying pan, add a teaspoon of oil and get the pan hot. Carefully add the scrapple, and cook to the desired doneness.
5. Toast the bagel, and butter it if you wish.
6. Place the scrapple and cheese-topped eggs on half the bagel. Top with the other half.

SUCCESS TIPS

• Cook the scrapple crispy on the outside and soft in the middle or flatten it with a spatula to make it crisp all the way through.

Serving Suggestion

▶ Add a splash of Texas Pete hot sauce.

Sambo's Tavern
283 Front Street
Leipsic, DE 19901
302.674.9724

Get Crackin' on the Leipsic: Sambo's Tavern

Standing by the bar, Elva Burrows keeps a keen eye on the door of Sambo's Tavern, the restaurant she owns with her husband, Ike. It's rare that she doesn't recognize a customer. "Hey, guys! How are you? Sit anywhere you want," she calls to two gentlemen who've stopped by for lunch. Shortly after their arrival, two ladies pause to chat before leaving. "Bye-bye, sweetheart, I'll see you later now. Thank you," Elva says as they step into the sunshine.

It's not surprising that Burrows knows her clientele. She and Ike have owned Sambo's for nearly 30 years.

The tavern, which is nestled next to the Leipsic River, was started in 1953 by Ike's father, Samuel "Sambo" Burrows, who grew up on a farm and became a crabber. Elva isn't sure what prompted him to buy the tavern. Perhaps, she says, it was because he had six children to feed. "He was a quiet man with a lot personality," she says. "He was so nice; he'd do anything for anybody."

Elva and Ike, who also spent time as a crabber, met through a mutual friend. When Ike's father talked about retiring, they decided to give the tavern a go rather than see him close it or turn it into apartments. "He rented it to us for a year and then we bought it," Elva says.

The tavern still buys only seasonal crabs from local watermen. (The restaurant closes from late October to early April.) The crabbers tie up at the dock just outside the restaurant, and the owners never know when they'll arrive or what size crabs they'll offer.

FUN FACT:

✫

A wall map in Sambo's has pins so you can mark your hometown. Take time to see how far some crab-fans have traveled.

✫

You might catch the action if you land a coveted seat by the windows, which look out over the idyllic river setting. These tables are so prized that some people won't stay if they can't get one. But the best seats are in the middle of the room, Elva maintains. Here, everyone at the table gets a view—not just those who face the window. Those who take her advice once tend to stick to the center.

The view, the rural drive and the history are good reasons for Sambo's enduring appeal. Yet the experience—smashing crabs on newspaper-covered tables while enjoying pitchers of beer with friends—as well as the consistent quality of the crab cakes, crab bisque, shrimp, chicken and steaks also bring them back for more. "We've been written up in the *New York Times* and the *Chicago Tribune*," Elva says.

Sambo's is no secret to the blue-crab happy set. Maine may have its lobster shacks, but Delaware has its Sambo's.

Steamed Crabs

Hot, juicy and sweet blue crabs are the state's favorite treat in summer. Not only do they provide a meal, but they also serve as a social occasion. Many people purchase them already steamed, but you can buy live crabs to steam yourself.

Prep Time:
10 minutes

Cook Time:
27 minutes

Makes a half-bushel (3 dozen crabs, depending on the size)

INGREDIENTS

A half-bushel of live crabs
1 quart of water
1 cup of apple cider vinegar
Seasoning of your choice, such as Old Bay or Sambo's own seasoning

PREPARATION

1. Place the crabs in a steamer insert, and place the insert in a stainless steel kettle.
2. Pour the water on top of the crabs, so that it gets them wet but drains out of the steamer and into the pot.
3. Add the vinegar on top of the crabs.
4. Sprinkle the seasoning on the crabs, as little or as much as you like.
5. Cook for 27 minutes. (If you have fewer crabs, reduce the time.)

SUCCESS TIPS

• Make sure to keep the crabs out of the water. You're steaming them, not boiling them.
• Pouring water and vinegar on top of the crabs helps the seasoning stick.

Serving Suggestion

▶ Serve with lemon, melted butter or vinegar for dipping.

▶ Provide mallets, crab knives and nutcrackers.

DELAWARE
CULINARY
TRAIL

Roma Italian Ristorante

3 President's Drive

Dover, DE 19901

302.678.1041

www.romadover.com

Ciao, Dover!: Roma Italian Ristorante

Home to the General Assembly, Dover Downs and the Dover Air Force Base, the state's capital has a diverse mix of residents and visitors. On any given day, you can see them mingle at Roma Italian Ristorante, a culinary fixture since 1973.

When business owners or civic groups aren't attending meetings in the banquet room, bridesmaids claim the space for showers. Over the years, legislators, including governors, have popped in for a power lunch. Roma is also a favorite among nearby air base personnel. In the evening, couples linger over tables draped in linens, while children celebrate birthdays in roomy booths for six. "We're a tradition," says owner Joseph Garramone. "It's affordable for families, but still elegant for special functions."

FUN FACT:

Veal saltimbocca, served over spinach, is a favorite at Roma. Saltimbocca, which also includes prosciutto, means "jumps in the mouth."

Like Dover, the restaurant has evolved over the years. Guiseppe Garramone, a native of Pietrapertosa, a small town in southern Italy, came to New York when he was 18. He later migrated to Newark, where he worked at a friend's pizzeria. Bitten by the entrepreneurial bug, he started hunting for his own location. He looked as far as Rehoboth, but it was still too sleepy in winter, so he purchased an old ice cream stand in Dover, near what was then the busy Blue Hen Mall.

Initially a one-room pizza place, Roma was so small you had to walk outside to access doors to the restrooms. Guiseppe expanded both the space and the menu. Despite the changes over the years, Roma still has the comfortable air of an independent red gravy house. You'd almost expect Frank Sinatra to stop by for a visit. "The longevity appeals to our customers," says Garramone.

Guiseppe was a stickler in the kitchen, Garramone says, and the menu features many of his original recipes. Garramone, who started working alongside his father at age 10, isn't afraid of garlic, and neither are his customers, who can't wait for the garlicky olive oil and fresh bread to hit the table.

Now retired, Guiseppe spends most of his time working in the garden and raising animals, just as he did as a boy growing up in Italy. He occasionally stops in the restaurant, but he trusts his son to run things, Garramone says. Sauces and stocks are still made in-house. Meat is butchered on-site. "This is the way we do things," Garramone says. "This is how it's always been done, and this is the way it will always continue."

Pasta with Broccoli Rabe & Grilled Sausage

Broccoli rabe, also known as rapini or broccoletti, gets its name from its appearance. Spiked leaves on long stalks surround a cluster of broccoli-like buds. The flavor, however, is decidedly different, ranging from nutty to slightly bitter. It pairs well with salty, savory sausage.

Serves: 2

Prep Time:
15 minutes

Cook Time:
40 minutes

INGREDIENTS

6-8 ounces of Italian sausage
1 bunch of broccoli rabe, about a half pound to a pound
14 ounces of chunky pasta, such as gemelli
½ cup roasted garlic
¼ cup extra virgin olive oil
½ cup diced plum tomatoes
Sea salt and cracked fresh pepper to taste
Grated Romano cheese

PREPARATION

1. Grill the sausage and slice on a bias. Set aside.
2. Cut and discard about 1 inch from each broccoli rabe stem.
3. In salted boiling water, cook the broccoli rabe until just tender, about 3 minutes.
4. Plunge the broccoli rabe into waiting ice water. Drain.
5. When the broccoli rabe is cool, roughly chop it up.
6. Cook the pasta according to directions, and drain over a bowl, reserving about 2 cups of the cooking water.
7. Sauté the roasted garlic in the olive oil.
8. Add broccoli rabe, tomatoes and just enough reserved water to create a sauce. Add more water as needed.
9. Add the grilled sausage and pasta. Stir.
10. Season with salt and pepper.
11. Divide into bowls and top with the cheese.

Serving Suggestion

▶ To make a sandwich, omit the pasta and put the vegetables and meat on a steak roll.

▶ Sprinkle with red pepper flakes, or serve them on the side.

Ingredient Substitution

▶ Use chicken broth instead of the pasta water.

Capriotti's Sandwich Shop
130 Gateway South Center, Route 10
Dover, DE 19901
302.698.3090
www.capriottis.com

A Homegrown Success: Capriotti's Sandwich Shop

Turkeys can't fly—at least, not very far. But Capriotti's Sandwich Shop, renowned for roasted turkey subs, has spread its wings, expanding its reach from Delaware to Pennsylvania to Maryland—even Las Vegas.

Capriotti's started in 1976 when Lois and Alan Margolet opened a Little Italy shop in Wilmington named for their mother's family. To differentiate themselves from other sub shops, the siblings offered fresh turkey subs, which they made from turkey that they roasted and shredded onsite. They started with one turkey a day, and soon they were roasting up to 12 turkeys a day to keep up with the sales.

Imagine roast turkey and you'll picture a Thanksgiving table laden with turkey, stuffing and cranberry sauce. Capriotti's tucks these holiday favorites on a roll. Named the Bobbie, this top-selling sandwich is available all year. The restaurant also sells cheesesteaks, Italian subs and specialty sandwiches, including the Capastrami: hot pastrami, Swiss cheese, Russian dressing and coleslaw on a sub roll.

The Bobbie is named for the founders' aunt, Bobbie, who used to take the Thanksgiving leftovers and make them sandwiches.

The Bobbie and other sandwiches began as local favorites, but word spread and people would travel hours just to taste a Capriotti's sub. To meet the demand, stores started popping up throughout Delaware, including Dover. The Margolets, who often visited their mother in Las Vegas, decided to open a restaurant there as well. Initially, it was a challenge: People out west didn't know what to make of the menu.

But the idea caught on, and Capriotti's sandwiches now win national awards. In 2009, for instance, Capriotti's tied the famous In-N-Out Burger for a first-place award in customer service, bestowed by Sandelman and Associates. Also that year, the Bobbie received the "Greatest Sandwich in America" honor by AOL/Lemondrop.

Delaware's celebrity sandwich shop is a destination in states throughout the country. Yet it still retains the neighborhood sentiment of that first Little Italy restaurant. "It's an honor for us to be on the Delaware Culinary Trail, because we think of ourselves as a First State phenomenon," says Ashley Morris, who purchased the chain in 2008. "We're still Capriotti's, where you feel like you're walking into a family-owned restaurant and grabbing a fresh, quality product."

The Bobbie

There's good reason why this renowned sub has won the "Greatest Sandwich in America." It's pure Americana on a roll. You can find it all year in a Capriotti's Sandwich Shop, but around Thanksgiving it's good football game-time grub to make at home with leftovers from your holiday feast.

Serves: 1

Prep Time:
5 minutes

Cook Time:
5 minutes

INGREDIENTS

1 fresh sub roll (9 inches, 12 inches or 20 inches, depending on your appetite)

Mayonnaise

Roast turkey, cooled, pulled from the bone and shredded not sliced

Favorite whole cranberry sauce

Salt and pepper

Homemade stuffing

PREPARATION

1. Slice the roll lengthwise, but don't slice all the way through. Leave a "hinge."

2. Spread mayonnaise on the top and bottom of the roll.

3. Add turkey to the bottom half.

4. Spoon the cranberry sauce evenly across the turkey.

5. Salt and pepper to taste.

6. Crumble homemade stuffing over the top.

SUCCESS TIPS

- Before shredding the turkey, remove the turkey from the pan and its juices so the turkey meat doesn't become too wet and mushy. (Save the broth and use it to make homemade soup or gravy.)
- Combine the white and dark meat evenly for a juicier and richer flavor.

Serving Suggestion

▶ Serve cold or at room temperature so the turkey doesn't dry out.

Cool Springs Fish Bar & Restaurant

2463 South State Street

Dover, DE 19901

302.698.1955

www.coolspringsfishbar.com

Riding the Wave: Cool Springs Fish Bar & Restaurant

As a child, Dennis Forbes was a picky eater, but not in the usual sense. Some children will only eat hamburgers, pasta or macaroni and cheese. Forbes was picky when it came to quality. His parents were excellent cooks, and they grew their own vegetables. Only a well-executed dish would do. He was equally picky when it came to consistency. When his aunt cut a sandwich diagonally instead of straight across like his mother did, he refused to eat it.

Those traits have served him well at Cool Springs Fish Bar & Restaurant, where the star, seafood, can be a temperamental ingredient in the wrong hands. Forbes, however, knew his way around a "striper" long before opening Cool Springs.

At age 13, he started working in his Dover neighbor's pizza place and diner. "Sometimes, I either want to thank or smack him," Forbes jokes. At 16, he moved to the Coral Reef Restaurant, a Dover seafood eatery. In 1985, he and a partner opened Plaza 9, which sold in 1997. He opened Cool Springs with his wife, Carolyn, in 1999.

> **FUN FACT:**
> ✫
> *Growing up in the Dover area, Forbes and his family always referred to the area where his restaurant is now located as "Cool Springs."*
> ✫

The cheerful restaurant, dressed in bright colors, keeps it simple and consistent. Rockfish, Chilean sea bass, cod and salmon might get a kiss of lemon and butter or a splash of cream sauce. Indeed, salt, pepper and lemon juice are his must-have ingredients. You'll also find Asian and French touches, such as wasabi and Newburg sauce. Happily, the kitchen takes an equally exacting approach to the steaks.

It's easy to feel like a local at Cool Springs. An overheard remark about your anniversary might earn you a dessert, and a couple might get a large table if there's a long wait for a two-top. Be prepared for a crowd; Cool Springs and its neighbor, Restaurant 55, which Forbes opened with daughter Desiree DiAntonio as he approached his 55th birthday, are popular. "It's not unusual to see the same customer in both restaurants on one night," Forbes says.

Belly-up to the bar, which curls around an open kitchen, and get dinner and a show. Forbes and his crew move like silvery minnows, darting from one task to the next. They vigorously shake a sauté pan, ladle sauce onto plates and pirouette between stations with ease and finesse.

Says Forbes: "Being a finicky kid has made me the finicky chef that I am today, and it's the reason why I love great food."

Pan-Fried Rockfish with Lemon-Butter Sauce

In the Delaware area, rockfish is also known as striped bass or "striper." It's a mild white fish that falls between meaty and flaky, making it incredibly versatile. You can fry it, poach it or bake it. This dish has been a top seller at Cool Springs Fish Bar & Restaurant since the restaurant opened.

Serves: 2

Prep Time:
10 minutes

Cook Time:
30 minutes

For the fish:

INGREDIENTS
2 8-10-ounce rockfish fillets, skin on
1 lemon wedge for the fish
Sea salt
1 cup of all-purpose flour
1 cup of milk
½ stick of unsalted butter
2 lemon wedges and parsley for garnish

PREPARATION
1. Squeeze lemon juice from 1 wedge onto the flesh of each rockfish fillet.
2. Lightly salt each fillet.
3. Dredge the flesh side of the fillet into the flour, then the milk, then more flour. (Do not flour or dredge the skin side.)
4. Melt ½ stick of butter over medium-high heat in a sauté pan that's large enough to accommodate the fish, and get the butter hot.
5. Place fish in the pan, flesh side down, and cook until lightly brown and crispy.
6. Flip, lower the heat and cook until the skin side is crispy and the fish is completely cooked.

For the sauce:

INGREDIENTS
¼ teaspoon of shallots, chopped
Extra virgin olive oil
2 ounces of dry white wine
1 lemon wedge
¼ teaspoon of Grey Poupon Dijon mustard
4 tablespoons of cold, unsalted butter, each dredged in flour, and kept ice cold until ready to use (½ stick cut into 4 tablespoons)

PREPARATION
1. Place ¼ teaspoon of shallots in small sauté pan, and just wet them with olive oil.
2. Sauté until the shallots start to lightly brown.
3. Remove from heat and add white wine, mustard and the juice from 1 lemon wedge. Whisk and return to heat.
4. Simmer the sauce, and add 4 floured butter patties, one at a time, until sauce starts to thicken. Do not boil. When the butter is incorporated, the sauce is done.

TO PLATE
1. Plate the rockfish and pour the sauce alongside the fish.
2. Garnish each plate with lemon wedge and fresh parsley.

SUCCESS TIPS

• Use a shallow pan or plate for the dredging.

Grotto Pizza
102 Silicato Way
Milford, DE 19963
302.725.5111
www.grottopizza.com

Swirl Sensation: Grotto Pizza

The son of Italian immigrants, Dominick Pulieri was just 13 years old when he stood on a milk crate so he could reach the pizza table at Joe's Pizza, the restaurant owned by his brother-in-law, Joseph Paglianite. The pizzeria, located in northeastern Pennsylvania, was famous for pies blanketed in rich sauce. Pulieri fell in love. As a teen working in the restaurant, he was equally enraptured by stories that a frequent customer told about sunny Rehoboth Beach in seemingly faraway Delaware.

In 1960, with visions of beach chairs dancing in their heads, Pulieri, then 17, his sister and his brother-in-law opened Grotto Pizza in Rehoboth Beach. They named the restaurant after The Grotto Bar, the business Paglianite had purchased and merged with his Pennsylvania pizzeria.

Pizza slices were 20 cents; a whole pie was $1.60. But Grotto Pizza initially fell flat. "Pizza wasn't as popular in 1960 as it is now," Pulieri says. "During the first summer, it was hard to even get people to try free samples because they didn't even know what pizza was."

Although Grotto became the darling of the tourists, it was the locals who were the first customers, he says. Curiosity simply got the better of them, and once they tasted Grotto's pizza, they were hooked. A second location opened on the boardwalk in 1963. Meanwhile, in the off-season, Pulieri got a degree from King's College in Wilkes-Barre, Pa., and he taught high school biology and chemistry until 1970.

> **FUN FACT:**
> ✴
> *The original Grotto pizza had a zigzag of sauce across the pie. But as the chain grew, the swirl design was easier to replicate.*
> ✴

During its first decade, the taste of a Grotto Pizza became as much a part of summer as fresh corn, tomatoes, beach fries, saltwater taffy and frozen custard. Open only from May to October, the restaurant built up a demand. By May, customers were eagerly awaiting opening day. They craved the thick sauce, slightly sweeter than most pizza sauces, and the chewy cheese, a special blend made in Wisconsin. The swirl delivers a different flavor profile with each bite. Some are cheesier, almost buttery; others are saucier. But you can sink your teeth into every one. When the season ended, they took pizza home to freeze and eat in fall and winter. "Guests tell us they take pizza home as far as Arizona!" Pulieri says. In 1974, Grotto became a year-round enterprise.

Today, there are 21 locations in Delaware, northeastern Pennsylvania and Ocean City, Md. Pulieri, who at 17 successfully marketed both a new restaurant and a new concept, is a master brander. All the locations are easily recognizable by their red-and-white color scheme, the chef's hat over the logo and the Mediterranean clock tower. The signature swirl appears at festivals, nonprofit events and fundraisers throughout the state. The menu has expanded beyond pizza to include pasta, sandwiches, appetizers, burgers, soups and calzones. Since 2007, Grotto has offered jarred pizza sauce and pasta sauce, as well as a bake-at-home pizza.

The pizza, though, is still the draw. The location and the season don't matter. Grotto's pizza is still a slice of summer sunshine in a box.

Bruschetta

While customers wait for their favorite Grotto Pizza to come to the table, they can nibble on this Italian antipasto. Pronounced "bru 'sketta," the appetizer showcases fresh ingredients. Make it after a visit to a local farmers market in summer.

Serves: 4-6

Prep Time: 20 minutes

INGREDIENTS
1 pound of plum tomatoes
1 ½ tablespoons of minced onions
1 ½ tablespoons of chopped fresh basil
Dash of pepper
1 teaspoon of salt or to taste
1 ½ teaspoons of minced garlic
2 tablespoons of extra virgin olive oil
1 loaf of Italian bread

PREPARATION
1. Wash the tomatoes under cold water.
2. Slice the core end off of each tomato, and dice the tomatoes.
3. Place tomatoes in a strainer to let the juices drain, about 1 hour.
4. Place drained tomatoes in a bowl, and add the onions, basil, pepper, salt, garlic and olive oil.
5. Gently blend all the ingredients together with a rubber spatula.
6. Slice and toast the bread.
7. Spoon the tomato mixture on each slice.

Serving Suggestion
▶ Add fresh mozzarella, spicy red pepper or cured meat to the mix.

Abbott's Grill
249 Northeast Front Street
Milford, DE 19963
302.491.6736
www.abbottsgrillde.com

Creative Cuisine on the Mispillion: Abbott's Grill

As a 12-year-old in Gainesville, Fla., Kevin Reading suffered defeat in a tennis match against an adult at his condominium community. Per the rules of the court, he had to wait a week before challenging his opponent again. "I waited seven days and one minute before knocking on his door," Reading says. Impressed with his spirit, the man offered Reading a dishwashing job in his restaurant.

From there, Reading climbed the culinary ladder. He shucked oysters, served as a maître d' and went to culinary school. He's opened not one but five restaurants, and he's never lost that drive or determination. "I'm about new ventures," he says. "I'm interested in starting things from scratch."

Good thing. He opened Abbott's Grill in 2009 just in time for a series of back-to-back snowstorms that brought local business to a halt. But the restaurant rebounded, becoming a hub for business lunches, celebratory dinners, after-work beers, bridal parties, jazz dinners and charity events.

Like his other endeavors, Abbott's Grill offers new American cuisine, only on a larger scale and with a more diverse approach. "Our mission here is to see people more often," Reading says. The multipurpose Abbott's has a contemporary but chic dining room, a pub with a plethora of flat screens, a private dining room and a patio with a Tuscan-style fireplace.

Before farm-to-table became a buzz phrase, Reading had made the practice his policy. At Abbott's, you might find Fifer Orchards pear salad or apple-scrapple flatbread. The bison burger and turkey sandwich are made with locally sourced meat. Just don't expect Reading to deliver the state's signature dishes just like mom used to make. Chicken-and-dumplings, for instance, features a European cut with pâte à choux gnocchi. Crispy chicken livers come with beet ketchup.

Reading might be ambitious, but you'd never know it by his low-key demeanor. While the pub and dining room each have their own menus, no one will quibble if you get a sandwich in the dining room. "We're so laid back," he says. "You can do whatever you want."

Game. Set. Match.

FUN FACT:

Kevin Reading founded the esoterically named Espuma and Nage, both in Rehoboth Beach. For his Milford eatery, he wanted a name that instantly resonated with area residents. Abbott is the name of an old gristmill, now the Abbott's Mill Nature Center, and a former shipbuilding yard.

Crab Cake with Sweet Corn Succotash

Delaware and the entire Delmarva Peninsula love crab cakes, which appear on casual and fine-dining menus alike. Abbott's Grill follows the Eastern Shore tradition of using Saltines, but the Imperial Sauce gives the cakes a signature spin.

Serves: 4
Prep Time: 45 minutes
Cook Time: 1 hour

For the succotash:

INGREDIENTS

4 ears of corn, shucked and roasted
1 pint of heavy cream
2 ounces of canola or vegetable oil
1 teaspoon of garlic, minced
1 cup of onion, diced small
½ cup of celery, diced small
½ cup of bell pepper, diced small
½ cup of peas, freshly shucked or frozen
½ cup of lima beans, frozen
½ cup of carrots, diced small
½ cup of white wine
1 tablespoon of sugar
1 teaspoon of oregano
3 dashes of Tabasco sauce
¼ cup of vinegar
Salt and pepper to taste

PREPARATION

1. Take the corn off the cob after roasting it.
2. Simmer the corn in the heavy cream for about 20 minutes. Strain and reserve the liquid.
3. Sweat onion, garlic, and celery in oil. Add bell pepper and cook for a few minutes.
4. Add the reserved corn cream, corn and all remaining ingredients. Simmer for up to 1 hour.

Serving Suggestion

▶ Garnish the crab cakes with the fresh herbs of your choice.
▶ Add a dollop of the tomato jam.

Ingredient Substitution

▶ Use edamame in place of lima beans.
▶ Use frozen corn instead of fresh.

For the tomato jam:

INGREDIENTS

1 tablespoon of water
1 teaspoon of gelatin
1 ounce of vegetable oil
1 teaspoon of fennel seed
1 cinnamon stick
Dash of cumin
Dash of ginger
Dash of allspice
½ cup of fennel, diced medium
½ cup onions, diced medium
1 clove of garlic, minced
1 teaspoon of shallot, minced
5 tomatoes, diced medium
½ cup of sugar
1 cup of cider vinegar
1 tablespoon of tomato paste

PREPARATION

1. Add water to gelatin, mix, and allow to gel. Set aside.
2. Heat oil in a small pan. Add fennel seed then cinnamon, cumin, ginger and allspice.
3. Add and sweat the fennel and onions over medium heat.
4. Add the rest of the ingredients, including the gelatin. Reduce heat to low.
5. Cook for 40 minutes until jam has a thick consistency.
6. Remove the cinnamon stick.
7. Chill before using.

SUCCESS TIPS

• Use a slotted spoon to put the succotash on the plate. You don't want too much liquid.

For the crab cakes:

INGREDIENTS

1 cup of Imperial Sauce (recipe below)
1 cup of Saltines, crushed
2 pounds of crabmeat
2 eggs, whisked
Canola or vegetable oil

PREPARATION

1. Combine Imperial Sauce and Saltines.
2. Fold in the crab carefully; don't break up the lumps.
3. Add eggs.
4. Form into 8 4-ounce portions. Chill in the refrigerator for 1-2 hours or overnight to set.
5. Add 1-2 tablespoons of oil to a nonstick pan. Brown crab cakes on medium-high heat 1-2 minutes on each side.
6. Transfer to a baking sheet and place in a preheated 350-degree oven. Cook for 5 minutes or until cooked through.

For the Imperial Sauce:

INGREDIENTS

2 egg yolks
1 cup of mayonnaise
1 teaspoon of dry mustard
¼ cup of red wine vinegar
1 tablespoon of lemon juice
1 tablespoon of Worcestershire sauce
3 shakes of Tabasco sauce
1 teaspoon of Old Bay to taste

PREPARATION

Combine ingredients and mix thoroughly.

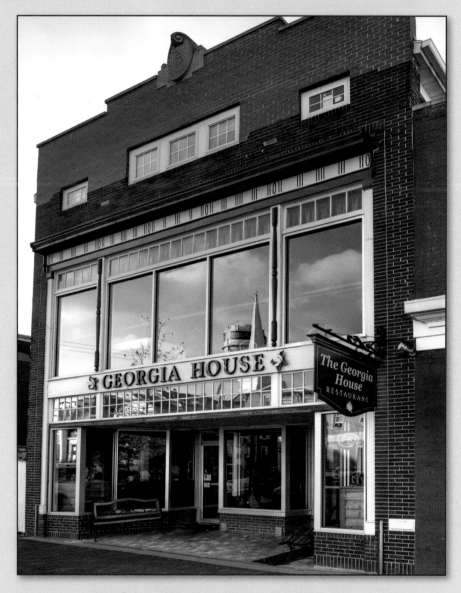

The Georgia House
18 South Walnut Street
Milford, DE 19963
302.422.6763
www.eatgh.com

Southern Hospitality: The Georgia House

The scent of classic home-style cooking emanates from the kitchen—meatloaf, fried chicken, steak. In between sips of sweet peach tea, the easy feel of a nice meal in one of Delaware's historic downtowns settles in.

This is comfort, and this is dinner at The Georgia House. For Kristal Hastings, the warm and cozy atmosphere is reminiscent of feasts on the Milton farm where she grew up. "My family always had huge dinners, and my grandmother was a great cook," she says. "She was very much into comfort foods like succotash and stewed tomatoes."

This highlight of Hastings' upbringing is now her bread and butter. Hastings is owner of the Milford and Millsboro locations of The Georgia House, and she's the general manager of all four Georgia House restaurants. (There are also locations in Selbyville and Laurel.)

The Georgia House was started in 1998 by Millsboro natives Larry McQuay and Shawn Hall, who've been friends since childhood. McQuay was working in a restaurant in Atlanta when Hall came to visit. They started talking about bringing Southern-style food to Sussex County, and the idea for The Georgia House was born.

In 2001, the Millsboro restaurant had outgrown its first location and moved up the street, and Hastings, who was also looking for growth and a relocation, came on board. Using her experience and training from culinary school in Pittsburgh, Hastings eventually took over the kitchen, offering specials inspired by her grandmother's dishes, before working her way up to manager and partner.

> **FUN FACT:**
> ✳
> *Miss Vicky's Meatloaf is named for a longtime worker who managed to grill the meatloaf slices without any cracks or holes. "It was perfect," Hastings says.*
> ✳

In 2006, the Milford site opened in the old Wiley Fuel and Appliances location, a landmark brick building that embodies small-town Main Street style and proudly boasts the charming battle wounds of a 2003 fire it survived thanks to good bones.

For the most part, the menus are the same. Cajun catfish, buttermilk fried chicken, Dallas chicken-fried steak and fried green tomatoes are served Southern-style. Strawberry-pretzel salad, however, is very Sussex County. At the restaurant, people buy the sweet dish as a side, a dessert and in bulk to take home for parties.

The Georgia House might be marching toward the north. "We would like to continue to grow," Hastings says. For now, this Delaware restaurant is content to serve down-home cooking with a smile.

Miss Vicky's Meatloaf

Meatloaf is pure comfort food, yet there are many variations. The Georgia House's version gets a pick-me-up from zesty barbecue sauce. Use your favorite, whether you like it spicy, smoky or sweet. This recipe is for a large family, or you can make two loaves and freeze one.

Serves: 10

**Prep Time:
1 hour**

**Cook Time:
1 hour, 20 minutes**

Serving Suggestion

▶ Go traditional with mashed potatoes and a green vegetable.

▶ Put sliced meatloaf on a good sub roll with fried onions and your favorite cheese.

Ingredient Substitution

▶ Use ground turkey or pork instead of beef.

INGREDIENTS

¼ cup of chopped garlic

4 cups of medium onion, diced

3 cups of celery, diced

1 ½ cups of green peppers, seeded and diced

¼ cup of Worcestershire sauce

Salt and pepper to taste

Granulated garlic to taste

2 ½ cups of half-and-half

2 ½ cups of tomato sauce

Cooking spray

3 ½ pounds of ground beef

3 eggs, whisked lightly

¾ cup of breadcrumbs

Barbecue sauce of your choice

Special equipment: Dutch oven

PREPARATION

1. Add the first seven ingredients to a Dutch oven. Cook, stirring over medium-low heat until vegetables just start to stick to the bottom of the pan.

2. Add half-and-half and tomato sauce.

3. Cook on low heat for about an hour, stirring occasionally, until the mixture is thickened and the liquid has been absorbed.

4. Let the mix cool and remove to a bowl. Refrigerate until completely cool.

5. Preheat the oven to 350 degrees, and line a baking sheet with foil. Spray the foil lightly with cooking spray.

6. In a large bowl, combine beef, eggs and the mix from the refrigerator. Add breadcrumbs in increments, and work the mix until it easily forms a ball. Mix until the ingredients are combined.

7. Place the mixture on the pan and form into a flat loaf about 1 ½ inches high. (You can make two loaves.)

8. Bake in the oven for 1 hour and 10 minutes or until cooked through.

9. Cool the meatloaf for about 10 minutes before slicing.

10. Brush with barbecue sauce and/or serve the sauce on the side.

Peach Bread Pudding

Peaches were once Delaware's dominant crop, and they're still a favorite fruit, especially when they're part of this sweet, soothing dish.

Serves: 10

Prep Time: 20 minutes

Cook Time: 40-45 minutes

INGREDIENTS

½ pound of butter

2 cups of sugar

8 eggs

1 tablespoon of cinnamon

1 tablespoon of vanilla extract

40 ounces of canned sliced peaches in syrup

1 loaf of white bread (80 ounces), diced

PREPARATION

1. Preheat oven to 350 degrees, and grease an 11-by-14 baking dish.
2. Microwave butter until just melted.
3. Put the sugar in a large bowl and whisk in the butter until the sugar dissolves.
4. Add eggs, cinnamon and vanilla.
5. Add peaches and bread.
6. Mix with a spatula until well combined and the bread is coated.
7. Pour into the baking dish.
8. Press down on the top to make the pudding level.
9. Bake for 40-45 minutes.
10. Let cool 10 minutes before serving.

Serving Suggestion

▶ Spoon the pudding in a bowl, top with vanilla ice cream and a dash of mixed sugar and cinnamon.

▶ Add a layer of gooey goodness by drizzling caramel sauce overtop of the pudding.

Jimmy's Grille

18541 South Main Street

Bridgeville, DE 19933

302.337.7575

www.deweybeachlife.com

Savoring Sussex County: Jimmy's Grille

The stars-and-stripes that snap in the wind in front of Jimmy's Grille tell the story. Surrounded by fertile farmland, the pale blue restaurant is a slice of Americana with an infusion of Sussex County flavor. The sign, meanwhile, leaves no doubt about the concept. The word "Family" is larger than the restaurant's name. Underneath: "Home Cooked Meals."

People don't come here to count calories, and a visit on any Saturday will demonstrate that. From the minute you walk in the door, a sign tells you to "Save Room for Dessert." If you need convincing, check out the towering dessert carousel, laden with three-layer cakes, fruit pies with basket-weave crusts and frothy meringue pies.

FUN FACT:

✫

Jimmy's is known as the home of the 3-pound cinnamon roll. In truth, a pack of six cinnamon buns weighs in at 2.25 pounds.

✫

A look around the diner reveals a diverse clientele. In one booth, a family from Washington, D.C., tucks into a rockfish sandwich, chicken salad paired with a crab cake and country-fried chicken breast. En route to the beach, they plan their annual trip so they can stop at Jimmy's both coming and going. And here is the local couple, married for 45 years, who regularly stop in for the fried chicken and breaded pork chop with gravy.

Each entrée comes with two sides. It's no easy choice. There are up to 15 on any given day, including corn pudding, collard greens, lima beans, cucumber salad, scalloped potatoes, strawberry-pretzel salad (only when fresh strawberries are available) and stewed tomatoes.

Jimmy's is old school, and that's why people love it. Tables have paper placemats with advertising printed on them. There are no flowers on the tables, only silverware and condiments.

Founded in 1993 by Jim Tennefoss, the restaurant was purchased in 2006 by beach-area restaurateur Alex Pires, who was attracted to the catering potential. (Jimmy's handles up to 900 offsite events each year.) With lots of parking, lots of guests and lots of catering trucks, it's a marked departure from his other restaurants. There are also lots of servers—at least 25—and most, he says, will call you "hon."

Slippery Dumplings & Chicken Gravy

Jimmy's Grille is famous for its fried chicken, the recipe for which is a closely guarded secret. Diners can order it alone or served atop slippery dumplings, one of Sussex County's signature dishes. Unlike traditional dumplings, this southern Delaware version is flat, so it gets nicely coated with chicken fat. It's a great dish to make with leftover roast chicken.

Serves: 4-6

Prep Time:
30 minutes

Cook Time:
15 minutes

Serving Suggestion

▶ Top with fried chicken or meat pulled from the bone of a roast chicken.
▶ Serve with lima beans and stewed tomatoes.

For the dumplings:

INGREDIENTS
3 ¾ pounds of flour
1 tablespoon of salt
2 tablespoons of shortening
3 ¾ cups of chicken broth

PREPARATION
1. Mix flour and salt.
2. Add the shortening with a pastry blender and blend well to create crumbs.
3. Gradually add the chicken broth and work the mix with your hands until it forms a dough. Avoid over-working the dough.
4. Flour a surface, such as a large cutting board.
5. Roll out the dough on the floured surface until it's about ⅛-inch thick.
6. Cut into 2-inch squares and refrigerate until chilled.
7. Heat water to a boil and add the dumplings.
8. Cook until dumplings are al dente, about 5 minutes.
9. Remove to serving bowl.

For the chicken gravy:

INGREDIENTS
1 cup of roast chicken drippings
1 ⅓ cups of flour
2 quarts of chicken broth, heated

PREPARATION
1. Heat the pan drippings in a pot.
2. Whisk in flour to create a roux. Continue whisking for 3-4 minutes.
3. In a separate pot, get the chicken broth hot.
4. Slowly stir in the hot chicken broth into the roux. Keep stirring until the gravy reaches the right consistency.

TO PLATE
Place cooked dumplings in a bowl, and add the gravy to cover. (You will have more than you need, so refrigerate the rest.)

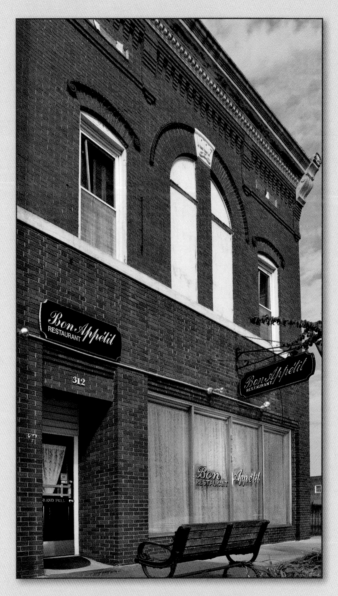

Bon Appétit

312 High Street

Seaford, DE 19973

302.629.3700

www.bonappetitseaford.com

Seaford's Gourmet Secret: Bon Appétit

The history behind this fine-dining icon stems from a love story that started in New York.

Culinary Institute of America graduate Karen Pedemonte grew up in the Big Apple, and Chino Pedemonte came to New York from Peru to chase the American dream. They fell in love while working at the same restaurant. The couple wanted to open their own place, but expenses in New York were too high. So they moved to the Eastern Shore, where her family lived.

Like any good love story, fate plays a part. While looking for work, Chino stumbled on a year-old restaurant in downtown Seaford. Instead of hiring Chino to work at the restaurant, the owner offered to sell it to him.

FUN FACT:

✴

Chino Pedemonte's home country, Peru, is a melting pot. Asian Peruvians comprise a significant portion of the population. Although he favors French preparations, Chino has been known to bring Incan, Chinese and Japanese flavors into the mix.

✴

And that's how this talented, cosmopolitan couple wound up in a charming small town in 1991.

The restaurant, Bon Appétit, now sets the stage for other love stories. Crisp white linen covers tables topped with fresh flowers. An imposing swag crowns the filmy curtains that filter light during lunch. As in a charming French café, walls are decorated with gilt-edged mirrors and prints.

The European sensibility also applies to the food, including escargot in garlic-butter and brandy, and a filet studded with black peppercorns. Expect French onion soup, quiche and a classic three-egg omelet. Yet you'll also find tuna salad, made with fresh tuna; a hamburger on French bread; and a chicken Caesar salad.

The restaurant is closed when Chino, the chef, isn't in the kitchen. "That's very European, and many people in New York restaurants work that way," Karen notes. They take Sundays and Mondays off, as well as a few weeks a year.

The practice means customers can count on consistency, which no doubt is why Bon Appétit remains a favorite after more than 20 years. For both Seaford and the Pedemontes, this tale has a happy—and flavorful—ending.

Poached Mussels & Sautéed Oysters

These classic dishes at Bon Appétit demonstrate the restaurant's devotion to French cuisine. Serve either as an appetizer or double the recipe for an entrée.

Serves: 2

Prep Time:
10 minutes

Cook Time:
15 minutes

For the poached mussels:

INGREDIENTS

20 mussels, cleaned
1 tablespoon of minced garlic
1 teaspoon of minced shallot
½ cup of white wine
2 tablespoons of whole butter
Salt and pepper to taste
½ cup of heavy cream at room temperature

PREPARATION

1. In a large saucepan, combine all ingredients except for the cream.
2. Cover and cook until the mussels open.
3. Place the cream in a separate bowl large enough to hold the mussels.
4. Pour the hot mussels and the sauce into the cream.
5. Divide into two bowls and serve.

For the sautéed oysters:

INGREDIENTS

1 tablespoon of clarified butter
1 tablespoon of minced garlic
1 teaspoon of minced shallot
1 tablespoon of minced herbs of
   your choice (dill, cilantro, basil)
10 shucked oysters

PREPARATION

1. Add butter to a sauté pan and cook the garlic, shallots and herbs.
2. Add the oysters and cook until the edges start to curl.
3. Divide into two bowls.

SUCCESS TIPS

- Serve both dishes with crusty bread.
- Always use fresh oysters or shuck them yourself.
- In addition to serving the oysters in a bowl, you can also pour them over prepared puff pastry.

Striper Bites

107 Savannah Road

Lewes, DE 19958

302.645.4657

www.striperbites.com

A Fresh Catch: Striper Bites

At 4 a.m., as most vacationers slept off the effects of the sun from the day before, Matt DiSabatino and his friends would sail out to the Delaware Bay, hanging bait on their fishing rods. By 10 a.m., they'd return to the DiSabatino family's summer home on Lewes Beach. Then, in the late afternoon, they'd head back to the bay, fishing sometimes until after sunset. Whenever one of them felt a tug on the line, others called out: "I think that's a striper bite!" or "It's a flounder biting!"

The excited cry of his youth became the inspiration for Striper Bites, the restaurant DiSabatino opened in 2001 in a 19th-century building in downtown Lewes. DiSabatino, who grew up working in restaurants from Dewey Beach to Lewes, plugged a niche for a casual yet high-energy eatery in one of his favorite towns. He also realized a goal: "I wanted to live at the beach," says the Smyrna native.

FUN FACT:

The wood bar and some furniture in the restaurant were made with reclaimed wood from the building's attic.

You'd never mistake Striper Bites for anything other than a seafood restaurant. The dinghy out front and the upside-down canoe suspended from the ceiling are giveaways. So are the fish prints, the fish sculptures, the ship's wheel and the tank of saltwater fish. The colorful décor is a little Key West and a little Nantucket. "We call it a nautical bistro," he says.

Locals and regulars come for the Striper Bites Club, made with blackened mahi mahi, bacon and Caesar dressing; crab cakes; sesame-encrusted tuna; and the "Local's Favorite," a tangle of penne pasta, tomatoes and blackened tuna in a fennel-cream sauce.

On a sun-splashed day, diners often opt for al fresco dining with a sidewalk view, or they escape the heat under a lazy paddle fan on the screened porch. The bar, however, is popular no matter the weather. While you wait for a seat, ignore the "Gone Fishing" sign on the hostess stand. DiSabatino is nearly always on hand, seating guests, pouring craft beer or delivering entrées. He enjoys catching up with regulars as much as they do. (If he's not there, he's likely at Kindle or Half-Full, the two Lewes restaurants he opened with chef Ian Crandall.)

"Striper Bites is one of those places that if you have a rough day, you can come here, decompress and lose yourself," he says. "If only for a little while." And in only a little while, you'll be hooked.

Spinach Salad with Grilled Salmon and Celery Seed Vinaigrette

From fried flounder sandwiches to crab bisque to crab cakes, seafood shines on the menu at Striper Bites. This spinach salad packs a lot of healthy flavors on the plate. Use the leftover vinaigrette as a poultry marinade.

Serves: 2

Prep Time: 20 minutes

Cook Time: 15 minutes

Ingredient Substitution

▶ Tuna, rockfish or shrimp can stand in for the salmon.

▶ Use dried cranberries in place of raisins.

▶ Use bleu cheese in place of feta.

For the vinaigrette:

INGREDIENTS

¾ cup of apple cider vinegar

2 teaspoons of dried mustard

1 teaspoon of kosher salt

6 ounces of honey

1 ½ teaspoons of celery seed

2 ½ cups of blended oil (typically a mix of canola and olive oil)

PREPARATION

1. Mix all the ingredients except for the oil in a mixing bowl.

2. Slowly whisk in the oil.

SUCCESS TIPS

• Make the dressing a day ahead and refrigerate to let the flavors mingle.

For the salmon and salad:

INGREDIENTS

2 7-ounce salmon fillets

Salt and pepper

Lemon wedge

1 tablespoon of melted butter

4 cups of fresh spinach leaves, washed and dried

1 cup of very loosely packed red onions, sliced

½ cup crumbled feta cheese

½ cup of gold raisins

¼ cup of toasted almonds

1 large Granny Smith apple, cored and cut into thin slices

Vinaigrette

PREPARATION

1. Season the fish with the salt and pepper, and drizzle with lemon juice and butter.

2. Grill the fish about 4 minutes on each side or to your liking.

3. Toss the spinach and the onions with enough dressing to coat. (Reserve the remainder for another use.)

4. Divide onto plates or into large bowls and sprinkle with remaining ingredients.

5. Top with the salmon.

DELAWARE
CULINARY
TRAIL

Nage

19730 Coastal Highway

Rehoboth Beach, DE 19971

302.226.2037

www.nagerestaurant.com

Everyday Gourmet: Nage

Traveling down Route 1 between Lewes and Rehoboth Beach, you might miss the small shopping center sandwiched between outlet shops. People with adventurous palates, however, know exactly where to turn to reach Nage. Since opening in 2004, the contemporary restaurant has gained a reputation for inventive cuisine that breaks the boundaries yet remains approachable. You're as likely to see people in jeans with sand in their sandals as you are diners in sports jackets.

The restaurant is also a mix of the casual and the sophisticated. Shiny glass tiles frame the open kitchen, and the dining room is dressed in warm earth tones: umber, green, burnt orange and beige. The wine preservation system in the comfortable wine bar lets Nage serve more than 30 wines by the glass.

This is the place for people who take their food seriously. Regulars can count on Nage "Classics," including the Nage burger, French onion soup and seafood stew in a tomato-saffron broth. The menu also showcases popular main ingredients, such as scallops and a crab cake. But they might get a friendly tweak each season. Take scallops with a Latin bean relish, ham and peanuts.

FUN FACT:

Cooking something à la nage translates to "while swimming" in French. It refers to a well-flavored broth.

Those who are undecided or who need more information need only ask the server, owner or even the chef, who gladly comes to the table. "Everybody who works at Nage is a foodie," says Josh Grapski, who founded Nage with well-known chef-restaurateur Kevin Reading. "Many of them have been in the restaurant business for years, and it's their calling."

Grapski is one of them. A graduate of both Cornell University's hotel administration program and The Restaurant School in Philadelphia, he's been in the industry since age 14. He worked as a sous chef in the banquet division of Le Cirque 2000, and he opened restaurants in California and New Orleans.

A key connection came while Grapski was in Restaurant School, where he met future business partner Reading. Grapski worked at Reading's first restaurant, located in Wilmington, and the two would reconnect just as Reading was opening his third restaurant, Nage, which debuted in spring 2004. Enchanted with the resort area, Grapski moved to Rehoboth the next year and joined Reading, and the two went on to open a second Nage location in Washington, D.C., in 2006. In 2010, Reading left Nage to dedicate himself to Abbott's Grill.

In 2012, Grapski debuted Root Gourmet, a café and to-go shop in the center next to Nage. "We're creating gourmet for foodies," Grapski says.

Nage Burger

Not just any burger, this decadent version gets a boost from mushroom duxelle, a finely minced mixture of mushrooms, onions and herbs that's usually associated with beef Wellington.

Serves: 6
Prep Time: 40 minutes
Cook Time: 1 hour

For the mushroom duxelle:

INGREDIENTS

½ pound of mushrooms, preferably morels but buttons will work

2 tablespoons of unsalted butter, divided

3 tablespoons of finely chopped shallots

Salt and pepper to taste

½ teaspoon of dried thyme or 1 ½ tablespoons of fresh thyme leaves

¼ cup dry vermouth, sherry or white wine

Special equipment: Food processor

PREPARATION

1. Finely chop the mushrooms in a food processor.

2. Scrape the mushrooms out into a clean, cotton towel.

3. Twist the towel around the mushrooms and wring out as much liquid as you can over the sink.

4. Heat a 10-inch nonstick skillet over a burner set between medium and medium-high.

5. Add 1 tablespoon of butter and swirl to melt. Avoid burning.

6. Add mushrooms, shallots, a pinch of salt, a pinch of black pepper and thyme. Stir frequently, until mushrooms appear dry and are beginning to brown, about 5 minutes.

7. Stir in remaining tablespoon of butter. When it's melted, add the vermouth, sherry or wine.

8. Cook, stirring frequently, until the vermouth has evaporated.

9. Remove from heat and cool.

For the smoked-pickled onions:

INGREDIENTS

1 cup of woodchips (apple wood preferred)

2 whole yellow onions or Vidalia onions, sliced

¼ cup of molasses

1 cup of cider vinegar

¼ cup of bourbon

¼ cup of sugar

⅛ cup of pickling spice

Special equipment: Smoker

PREPARATION

1. Follow your smoker's directions and smoke the onions for about an hour.

2. Remove onions and place them in a bowl.

3. Bring the rest of the ingredients to a boil and immediately pour over the onions.

4. Place the mix in the refrigerator for 12 to 24 hours.

For the burger:

INGREDIENTS

2 pounds of ground steak from the butcher

¼ cup of mushroom duxelle

¼ cup of fresh ground Parmesan cheese

1 capful of Worcestershire sauce

3 shakes of Tabasco sauce

1 teaspoon of garlic powder

1 teaspoon of dry oregano

½ teaspoon of black truffle oil

Salt and pepper to taste

Smoked onions, as many as you wish, for each burger

12 slices of Gouda

6 quality rolls

PREPARATION

1. Mix the first 9 ingredients in a bowl.

2. Portion into 6-ounce portions and make patties.

3. In a hot skillet, sear each side of the burgers until they're brown on both sides.

4. Place the seared burgers in a preheated 400-degree oven and cook to your desired temperature.

5. Remove the burgers, top each with onions and 2 slices of cheese and return to the oven. Cook until the cheese melts.

6. Place on buns and serve.

SUCCESS TIPS

• Use an old cotton towel for the mushroom duxelle as it will stain the towel. Do not use terrycloth.

Serving Suggestion

▶ Nage serves the burger with its fries and tomato jam, which you can buy at Root.

The Cultured Pearl Restaurant & Sushi Bar

301 Rehoboth Avenue

Rehoboth Beach, DE 19971

302.227.8493

www.culturedpearl.us

Jewel in the Crown:
The Cultured Pearl Restaurant & Sushi Bar

Susan Townley Wood, the owner of one of Delaware's premier restaurants for sushi, actually didn't like the bite-sized Japanese fare the first time she tried it in 1991. "I was hungry afterward," she recalls. "Where were the meat and potatoes?" But she couldn't get it out of her mind. "I found myself craving it, so I went back and tried it again."

The second time was the charm. Wood, who then lived in Ocean City, Md., became a self-professed sushi addict, driving to either Annapolis or Philadelphia every few weeks to visit friends and eat sushi. Finally, she asked a sushi chef in Philly if he'd come work for her if she opened a Rehoboth Beach restaurant. It wasn't such a stretch. Wood at the time owned a drafting and design business and expedited building permits. Restaurants were among her clients.

The sushi chef agreed, and The Cultured Pearl opened in 1993 in a former clothing shop storeroom. Wood had her hands full. Three days before opening, she'd fired the kitchen chef, who liked drinking more than cooking. "I wound up being the kitchen chef, and I didn't really cook," Wood says. Fortunately, sushi was the draw, and the sushi chef helped out with the cooked Japanese items. She handled steaks, pasta and American "backup" dishes for non-sushi fans.

FUN FACT:

✦

In 1994 and 1995, when The Cultured Pearl closed in Rehoboth Beach for winter, it moved operations to Telluride, Colorado, to keep chefs employed all year long.

✦

Business caught on, and Wood expanded, tripling in size between 1997 and 2003. Meanwhile, she met and married Rob Wood, a Vancouver native. Although he worked in computers when they met, he wound up in the kitchen. "When you own a restaurant, you do a little of everything," he says. He even learned to make sushi.

The Cultured Pearl is now located in an imposing 22,000-square-foot, second-floor space in a Rehoboth landmark, the former Quillen's Hardware store.

The restaurant is fitted with awe-inspiring Asian-influenced water features and décor. Inside, guests dine within a lush bamboo garden featuring a fish pond that weaves throughout the room. The showstopper is on the outdoor deck—a 15,000-gallon, koi-filled "lake" surrounded by gazebos for dining.

Still known for sushi, the "Pearl" recently beefed up its Japanese-inspired entrées. Wood has added Korean barbecue and Thai dishes. However, there's a seafood pasta with penne dish that "we can never take off the menu," Wood says. After 20 years, you'd think her love affair with sushi would wane. That's not the case. "We have so many rolls and selections—and it's good for you," she says. "I've never gotten tired of it."

Rehoboth Roll

The Rehoboth Roll is designed for the serious sushi eater. It consists of the big three sushi fish: tuna, salmon and yellowtail. Flying fish eggs add a contrast of color and texture. You will need a maki-su, also known as a sushi mat or rolling mat.

Serves: 4

Prep Time: 30-40 minutes

INGREDIENTS

1 12-ounce container of seasoned rice from a Japanese restaurant
½ pound of tuna
½ pound of salmon
½ pound of yellowtail
4 nori sheets
2 avocados
2 ounces of flying fish eggs
1 bottle of soy sauce
Wasabi paste (as needed)
Pickled ginger (as needed)

PREPARATION

1. Slice the fish lengthwise in pieces about ½-inch thick.

2. Pit, quarter and peel the avocados.

3. Slice the avocados lengthwise in even widths, about ¼-inch thick.

4. Place a piece of nori, rough side up, horizontally on a dry cutting board.

5. Take a handful of sushi rice (about half the size of a tennis ball) and place evenly across the entire sheet of nori. Leave a ½-inch space bare along the top edge. Make sure the rice extends all the way to the left, right and bottom edges. Don't push down too hard on the rice.

6. Flip the nori so that the smooth side, without the rice, is face up and the ½-inch strip is down and toward you.

7. Place the fish horizontally along the length of the nori. Keep all the slices about ⅓ of the way up from the bottom edge of the nori. Stack the fish on top of one another.

8. Gently roll the edge closest to you up and over the fish. Give a slight squeeze, and then roll it the rest of the way around.

9. Use the maki-su to gently squeeze the roll and make it uniform. Place the maki-su over the top of the roll, and apply slight pressure along the length of the roll. (Pushing too hard will force your fish out each end.)

10. Remove the maki-su, and place the avocado slices, with a slight overlap, down the length of the roll.

11. Place a sheet of plastic film over the avocado and the roll, and then place the maki-su on top. Gently apply pressure to make the avocado take the shape of the roll on the top and the sides.

12. Remove the maki-su and the plastic film from the roll.

13. Cut the roll into 8 equal pieces.

14. Place on a plate and top with flying fish eggs.

15. Serve with soy, wasabi and pickled ginger.

Ingredient Substitution

▶ Substitute any fish or protein for the salmon, tuna and yellowtail. You can also use your choice of vegetables.

▶ You can sear the fish instead of using completely raw fish.

SUCCESS TIPS

- Find ingredients for the Rehoboth Roll at major supermarkets and Asian grocery stores.
- When consuming raw fish, it's best to source it from a reputable fishmonger. Using fresh is best, so tell the fishmonger that you're making sushi and eating it raw.
- Sushi means "seasoned rice," so only buy it already seasoned. Regular rice won't offer the same flavor.

Big Fish Grill

20298 Coastal Highway

Rehoboth Beach, DE 19971

302.227.3474

www.bigfishgrill.com

A Fresh Catch: Big Fish Grill

Y ou don't need a calendar to tell you it's a weekend in summer. Just drive by Big Fish Grill on Route 1. In addition to the cars crowding the lot, you'll inevitably see people waiting for a table. Once inside, the restaurant is hopping, with servers a blur as they zip between customers, writing their names on the paper that covers the tables.

Big Fish Grill, which opened in 1997, is a destination for diners seeking fresh seafood at affordable prices. Customers crave the baked oysters, flash-fried flounder, crab cakes and daily fish specials. You'll also find thick burgers and roast chicken.

Owners and brothers Norman and Eric Sugrue based the friendly concept on their family gatherings. The Sugrues, who moved to Rehoboth Beach in 1977, seldom lacked for hungry visitors who appreciated home cooking. (The recipe for Neva's potatoes comes from the Sugrue matriarch, Geneva.)

During their teenage years, the brothers worked in restaurants, but they studied business in college. The hospitality industry, however, has a strong pull. "We both worked in many restaurants and felt it was the right path," Eric Sugrue says. While Norm polished his skills in restaurant kitchens, he gained management experience in major restaurant chains, including the Cheesecake Factory.

FUN FACT:

★

The market sells just about everything the cooks use in the restaurant kitchen, including Big Fish's own Steak Spice. Along with steak, use it on fish, french fries and mashed potatoes.

★

The brothers targeted Rehoboth Beach as a location for their restaurant because it's where they spent their childhood, and Norm wanted to raise his family there. As a concept, seafood was a natural. But what to call it? "We thought of every type of fish or seafood for a name—Grouper, etc.," Sugrue recalls. He'd worked near a restaurant in Nashville called Big River, which gave Norm the idea for Big Fish. To open the restaurant, the brothers pooled their money, borrowed from family and secured a loan.

Big Fish is decorated with mounted fish against a blue ceiling. Some wear whimsical dairy cow prints (as do the ceiling fans). It's light, open and, on a busy night, buzzing with the sounds of friends and families.

When owners ran out of space to cut the fish, they bought the building next door for a fish-cutting area. "Then we realized people wanted to buy our raw product, so we decided to turn it into a seafood market," Sugrue recalls. "As the years progressed, we were overwhelmed by the amount of people who wanted cooked items." The fish-cutting area moved to a building in the back. The market has a dedicated kitchen for takeout and a 50-seat patio.

Although the restaurant now has locations in Wilmington and Pennsylvania, the headquarters remains in Rehoboth Beach. "We are so fortunate to be in Sussex County," Sugrue says. "It is a great place to live and do business."

Cioppino

Cioppino is often associated with San Francisco, home to a large population of Portuguese- and Italian-Americans. The fishermen who immigrated to the bay area would pool leftovers to make a stew, and the name reportedly comes from the command to "Chip in!" More likely, it's a variation of ciuppin, a similar dish in Genoa. Big Fish Grill's version includes pasta.

Serves: 1

Prep Time:
15 minutes

Cook Time:
40 minutes

Serving Suggestion

▶ Sprinkle with chopped basil.

▶ Put fresh grated parmesan on the side.

▶ Serve with garlic bread.

Ingredient Substitution

▶ You can use any mix of seafood you wish, but a white fish is best.

INGREDIENTS

¾ of a stick of unsalted butter
¼ cup of chopped garlic
¼ cup of chopped shallots
16 ounces of clam juice
2 ½ cups of marinara sauce
2 ½ cups of chopped stewed tomatoes
1 cup of white wine
2 tablespoons of chicken base or
   10 tablespoons of chicken stock
4 cloves of roasted garlic
Salt and pepper to taste
1-2 teaspoons of extra virgin olive oil
3 jumbo shrimp
3 large sea scallops
6 Prince Edward Island black mussels
4 middle-neck clams
4 ounces of white fish pieces, such as cod
8 ounces of Barilla pasta

PREPARATION

1. Melt butter in a large saucepan and sauté garlic and shallots until translucent.

2. Add clam juice, marinara sauce, tomatoes, white wine, chicken base or stock and the whole cloves of garlic.

3. Bring to a simmer and season as needed.

4. In a sauté pan, add the olive oil and sear the shrimp, scallops, fish, mussels and clams.

5. Add 12 ounces of the sauce-broth mixture to the seafood pan, and simmer until mussels and clams open.

6. Meanwhile, boil water and cook the pasta according to directions. Drain well.

7. When the pasta and seafood are done, mix everything together in the large saucepan.

Bluecoast Seafood Grill
30904 Coastal Highway
Bethany Beach, DE 19930
302.537.0100
www.bluecoastseafoodgrill.com

A Room with a View: Bluecoast Seafood Grill

Like a curtain at a command performance, the tinted sheer shade in the dining room slowly rises. Almost as one, all eyes turn toward the window. The sun—a ball of orange, yellow and red—is preparing to set, sending gold streaks across the verdant marsh grass and indigo bay. Forks pause in midair and necks stretch as diners seek a better view.

The sunset is a star attraction each evening at Bluecoast Seafood Grill, but it's not the only one. Since it opened in 2001, the restaurant has consistently ranked as one of the beach's best attractions, earning rave reviews from *The Washington Post* and major travel publications.

Bluecoast is the baby of celebrated local chef Matt Haley, a Washington, D.C., native who spent summers with his four siblings at the beach, enjoying local corn, sun-ripened tomatoes and shucked oysters. But the oldest "child" now has plenty of company. Haley also owns Fish On in Lewes, Lupo di Mare in Rehoboth Beach, Northeast Seafood Kitchen in Ocean View, Matt's Fish Camp just up the road in North Bethany and Catch 54 in Fenwick Island.

FUN FACT:

☆

Owner Matt Haley in 2012 received the Cornerstone Award from the Delaware Restaurant Association, a lifetime achievement award that honors the restaurant, hospitality business or individual who has added prestige to the hospitality industry.

☆

The common theme: Fresh ingredients whose flavors are allowed to shine. "I believe strongly that we need to support the purveyors in our own community," says Haley, who is also known for his philanthropy. "We're incredibly fortunate in Sussex County to have a number of dedicated farmers, and we have some of the best farmers markets in the country."

Bluecoast is famous for its tempura-fried or baked Chincoteague Oysters, pan-roasted jumbo shrimp and seafood stew. You'll also find grilled veal meatloaf and a New York strip adorned with a sunny-side-up egg, tomato-veal gravy and Parmesan herb fries.

It's all served in a contemporary atmosphere with white walls, modern art, classic wood chairs and black booths. The spare yet sophisticated design showcases Mother Nature, visible through the many windows.

Bluecoast has withstood storms, both in winter and summer, and competition from newcomers. Yet more than 10 years after its founding, its prices have stayed steady and its ingredients remain top-notch. Vacationers often visit more than once during their stay for the consistent food, the ambiance and the service.

The show-stopping sunset is the icing on top.

Lobster Cavatappi

Mix comfort food with a dash of sophistication and you've got a dish that will make you feel warm, satisfied and wonderfully decadent.

Serves: 4-6

Prep Time:
15 minutes

Cook Time:
25 minutes

INGREDIENTS

1 pound of cavatappi
1 quart of heavy cream
8 ounces of whole milk
8 tablespoons of unsalted butter
½ cup of all-purpose flour
18 ounces of shredded sharp white cheddar cheese
½ teaspoon of ground white pepper
½ teaspoon of ground nutmeg
1 tablespoon of vanilla extract
1 ½ pounds of cooked lobster meat (from about 3 lobsters)
2 cups of fresh green peas

PREPARATION

1. Boil water in a large pasta pot. Add the pasta and cook according to the directions. Drain well.

2. In a small saucepan, heat the milk and cream but do not boil.

3. In a larger pot, melt the butter and whisk in the flour. Cook for 2 minutes, stirring constantly.

4. While still whisking, slowly add the hot cream. Cook until thickened and smooth, about 3-4 minutes.

5. Take the cream off the heat. Whisk in shredded cheese, pepper, vanilla and nutmeg.

6. Stir in the cooked pasta, lobster meat and peas.

7. Divide into 4 to 6 dishes and serve.

Ingredient Substitution

▶ If you can't find cavatappi, use any hollow pasta, including macaroni, penne or ziti.

▶ You can use frozen peas instead of fresh.

DELAWARE CULINARY TRAIL

BETHANY BEACH . SUSSEX COUNTY

DiFebo's
789 Garfield Parkway
Bethany Beach, DE 19930
302.539.4550
www.difebos.com

A Family Affair: DiFebo's

DiFebo's, located a mile from the ocean, is a labor of love in more ways than one. Lisa DiFebo-Osias launched the business in 1989 as a 40-seat deli/café partly because the Wilmington native hated to leave the beach, where her family had a second home. "We served subs and steaks with some family specialty sandwiches, pasta and homemade meatballs with my father's Sunday gravy," she recalls.

Yet she was always "pushing the envelope" by adding a pan-roasted veal chop or an inventive fish dish. Customers, including sophisticated vacationers from urban hubs, showed their appreciation. Encouraged, DiFebo-Osias enrolled at the Culinary Institute of America. On weekends, she commuted five hours back to the beach to work in her restaurant, and she returned to New York on Sunday for Monday morning classes. She even managed an externship at an Italian restaurant in Florida, run by a Tuscan chef. "I was an owner, an employee and a student all at once," she says.

Her time in culinary school also paid dividends in her personal life, as she ended up marrying one of her classmates, Jeff Osias. Married in 1996, the couple took DiFebo's from a small café to a 125-seat restaurant. By 1998, the eatery was scooping up best restaurant awards in southern Delaware.

Whether customers come once a week or once a summer, they can count on antipasto with paper-thin slivers of prosciutto and penne pasta with San Marzano tomatoes and fresh basil. Pesto-crusted lamb chops, still blushing pink, curl next to prosciutto-sage risotto. Tender chicken Marsala is perched next to a mound of whipped potatoes. Frequent specials, including early-bird deals, ensure repeat business. It's all served either in the Mediterranean-inspired dining room or al fresco under the sun or stars.

> **FUN FACT:**
> ✮
> *DiFebo's nearly always has tiramsu on the menu. Italian for "pick me up," the espresso-based dessert is often eaten as an afternoon snack in Italy.*
> ✮

In 2008, the 100-seat DiFebo's Bistro at Bear Trap Dunes Golf Club opened in nearby Ocean View.

Jeff and Lisa now have three children, but the two restaurants are considered part of the family. "We truly have a lot on our plate, but we relish the opportunity and privilege of running a household and two restaurants," she says.

Tuscan Veal Chop with Potatoes and Asparagus

Italian cuisine goes far beyond red sauce and pasta. Witness this Tuscan-inspired dish that gets rave reviews at DiFebo's in Bethany Beach. Veal demi-glace adds flavorful depth.

Serves: 4
Prep Time: 20 minutes
Cook Time: 45 minutes

For the potatoes:

INGREDIENTS

6 potatoes, peeled and washed
⅓ cup of heavy cream
2 tablespoons of butter
1 teaspoon of white pepper
Salt to taste

PREPARATION

1. Place peeled potatoes in a pot, cover with well-salted water and add about 2 tablespoons of salt.

2. Bring to boil and cook for about 15 minutes or until the potatoes are tender.

3. Strain and return to the pot.

4. Add cream, butter and white pepper. Mix or whip thoroughly. Add salt if needed. Place in a bowl and keep warm.

Ingredient Substitution

▶ Substitute chicken or beef stock for the veal stock.

For the asparagus:

INGREDIENTS

20-30 fresh asparagus spears
Salt

PREPARATION

1. Cut about 1 ½ inches off the bottom of each spear.

2. Bring a small pot of salted water to a boil and fill a bowl with ice water.

3. Boil the asparagus for 1 minute. Drain and instantly place in the ice water to halt cooking.

4. After about 3-4 minutes, remove from the ice water. Reserve.

For the veal chops:

INGREDIENTS

4 12-ounce "Frenched" center-cut veal chops
Salt and pepper to taste
4 teaspoons of rosemary powder, a finely ground, dry rosemary spice
1 tablespoon extra virgin olive oil
3-4 portobello mushroom caps, sliced
1 cup of veal stock
1 tablespoon of veal demi-glace
1 tablespoon of butter
Reserved asparagus
2 tablespoons of water
1 teaspoon of white truffle oil

PREPARATION

1. Rinse the veal chops and pat dry.

2. Season both sides of the veal chops well with salt, pepper and powdered rosemary.

3. Add 1 tablespoon of extra virgin olive oil to a sauté pan, and get it very hot. Place veal chops in the pan. Sear each side for about 1 minute each.

4. Remove the chops and place on sheet tray. Place in preheated 350-degree oven, and cook for 12-15 minutes.

5. While the chops are in the oven, reheat the sauté pan on high heat. Add mushrooms. Sauté for 3 minutes.

6. Add veal stock and let it boil. Add demi-glace and let it dissolve.

7. Bring the sauce to a boil, then reduce heat. Simmer until the liquid is reduced by half or until thick.

8. Pour into gravy boat and reserve.

9. Return the pan to the heat. Add 1 tablespoon of butter and the cooked asparagus. Add 2 tablespoons of water to "steam" the asparagus, creating a sauce with the gravy remnants from the bottom of the sauté pan.

TO PLATE

1. Place potatoes toward the back of each plate.

2. Carefully lean the veal chop, bone facing away, on the potatoes.

3. Pour the veal gravy over the chop, so it cascades toward the front of the plate.

4. Place the asparagus on each plate, leaning them on the chop's bone. Add a drizzle of white truffle oil over the asparagus.

SUCCESS TIPS

• Ask your butcher to cut the chops for you, and make sure they're bone-in, which gives them more flavor.

• Buy good quality truffle oil; it makes a difference in the taste. Only use a drizzle; a little bit goes a long way.

• Veal demi-glace is available in many specialty shops or online.

NEW CASTLE COUNTY

1 Harry's Savoy Grill
2 Claymont Steak Shop
3 Charcoal Pit
4 Green Room at Hotel du Pont
5 Piccolina Toscana
6 Walter's Steakhouse
7 The Dog House
8 Deer Park Tavern

KENT COUNTY

9 Smyrna Diner
10 Sambo's Tavern
11 Roma Italian Ristorante
12 Capriotti's Sandwich Shop
13 Cool Springs Fish Bar & Restaurant
14 Grotto Pizza
15 Abbott's Grill
16 The Georgia House

SUSSEX COUNTY

17 Jimmy's Grille
18 Bon Appétit
19 Striper Bites
20 Nage
21 The Cultured Pearl Restaurant & Sushi Bar
22 Big Fish Grill
23 Bluecoast Seafood Grill
24 DiFebo's

DELAWARE
CULINARY
TRAIL

Index

First State Plates:
Iconic Delaware Restaurants and Recipes

Pam George, First State Plates Writer

Pam George has been writing about food for more than 15 years. She has explored wine, steakhouses, desserts and crab dishes for *Delaware Today*, and she regularly writes a recipe column for *Delaware Beach Life*. Her work has also appeared in *Fortune, Men's Health, US Airways Magazine* and *Go!*, the in-flight magazine for AirTran. She is the author of "Shipwrecks of the Delaware Coast: Tales of Pirates, Squalls & Treasure" and "Landmarks & Legacies: Exploring Historic Delaware."

Keith Mosher, Photographer

Keith Mosher is the owner and photographer of KAM Photography, established in 2002. Keith earned a Bachelor of Fine Arts degree with a concentration in photography from Shepherd University in 2001. Keith shoots commercial and editorial work, including the 2012-2014 Delaware Travel Guide, and also does weddings and portraits. His career has taken him on assignments all around Delmarva into cities such as Washington, D.C., New York City, and to Mexico. When he is not shooting for clients, he concentrates on black-and-white photography, which has been exhibited in numerous galleries. He also teaches digital photography courses at Delaware Technical Community College, Owens Campus.

Heather Kenton, Tourism Development Leader, Delaware Tourism Office

Heather Kenton serves as the Tourism Development Leader for the Delaware Tourism Office, focusing on consumer initiatives. Heather promotes overnight stays and encourages visitors to enjoy the unique experiences that Delaware has to offer. She organized Delaware's first state-sponsored Geocaching Trail, the Delaware History Trail and the popular Delaware Wine and Ale Trail. In her previous role as Group Tour Development Leader, she implemented the Delaware Motorcoach Rewards Program and managed the development of the Delaware Loves Buses sales and marketing video. A graduate of the University of Delaware, Heather obtained her Bachelor of Science degree in Psychology and currently resides in Rehoboth Beach, Del.

Peter Bothum, Marketing & Public Relations Coordinator, Delaware Tourism Office

Peter Bothum spent 15 years as an award-winning newspaper reporter and editor, covering everything from hard news and business to music, food and the arts. After graduating from the University of Delaware in 1997, Peter went on to work at three papers in Pennsylvania, including six years at the *York Daily Record*, where he wrote an award-winning three-day series on restaurant cleanliness. Prior to coming to the Delaware Tourism Office, Peter spent seven years at *The News Journal*, Delaware's largest newspaper, and served as editor of the paper's weekend entertainment section.